Cambridge First Certificate in English 6
with Answers

D0494136

Cambridge First Certificate in English 6

WITH ANSWERS

Examination papers from University of Cambridge ESOL Examinations: English for Speakers of Other Languages

CAMBRIDGE UNIVERSITY PRESS

PUBLISHED BY THE PRESS SYNDICATE OF THE UNIVERSITY OF CAMBRIDGE
The Pitt Building, Trumpington Street, Cambridge, United Kingdom

CAMBRIDGE UNIVERSITY PRESS
The Edinburgh Building, Cambridge CB2 2RU, UK
40 West 20th Street, New York, NY 10011–4211, USA
477 Williamstown Road, Port Melbourne, VIC 3207, Australia
Ruiz de Alarcón 13, 28014 Madrid, Spain
Dock House, The Waterfront, Cape Town 8001, South Africa

http://www.cambridge.org

First published 2003
Third printing 2004

Printed in the United Kingdom at the University Press, Cambridge

ISBN 0 521 75444 5   Student's Book (with answers)
ISBN 0 521 75443 7   Student's Book
ISBN 0 521 75446 1   Teacher's Book
ISBN 0 521 75447 X   Set of 2 Cassettes
ISBN 0 521 75448 8   Set of 2 Audio CDs
ISBN 0 521 75445 3   Self-Study pack

Contents

Thanks and acknowledgements

The publishers are grateful to the following for permission to reproduce copyright material. Whilst every effort has been made to locate the owners of copyright, in some cases this has been unsuccessful. The publishers apologise for any infringement or failure to acknowledge the original sources and will be glad to include any necessary correction in subsequent printings.

Times Newspapers for the text on p.3 'Speeding Over Seas' by Jennai Cox from *The Times Wild Spirits Supplement*, 25 April, 1998, for the text on p.55 'Facing the Truth' from the *Brainpower Supplement, The Sunday Times*, February, 1998, and for the text on p.98 'See you in three years says jogger on lap of the world' by Russell Jenkins, *The Times*, 7 December, 1996. © NI Syndication Limited, London; Constable & Robinson Limited for the texts on pp.4 and 30 from *Cross my Heart and Hope to Die* by Sheila Radley, 1992; *The Illustrated London News* for the text on p.9 by Jo Foley, 1998; *New Scientist* magazine for the text on p.29 'The Big Yawn', by Amy Adams, December 1988, © RBI 1988; Mike Bell for the text on p.32 'Living in the Valley' from *Peak and Pennine*, March, 1998; IPC Syndication for the texts on pp.35 and 87 by Nina Hathway, 'Confident people, what's their secret?' from *Woman's Weekly*, February 1997, and 'Variations on a Theme' from *Woman's Weekly*, July, 1996, © Nina Hathway/*Woman's Weekly*/IPC Syndication; *The Independent* for the text on p.56 'The Shell Artist' by Peter Cooke, 27 April, 1996, and for the text on p.82 'Film Critic' by Mark Adams, 11 October, 1996; the Editor of *Caterer & Hotelkeeper* for the text on p.58 from the article 'Chips with everything', 29 January, 1998; New Holland Publishers (UK) Limited for the adapted text on p.72 from *Secret London* by Andrew Duncan, 1995; Rose Rouse for the text on p.84 from the article 'Fun at the Dentist's, *The Guardian*, 31 December, 1996.

For permission to reproduce copyright photographs:

Art Directors & TRIP/C Kapolka for p.32, /J Greenberg for p.C1 (bottom), /Helene Rogers for p.C6 (top left), /J Stanley for p.13 (top), /B Gadsby for p.13 (bottom), /S Grant for p.C16 (top); John Birdsall Photography for pp.C5 (bottom), C12 (bottom),

C15 (bottom left); Getty Images/Stewart Cohen for p.C5 (top), Don Johnston for p.C7 (top), /John Warden for p.C7 (centre), /Alan Klehr for p.C8 (top), /E Dygas for p.C8 (bottom), /Howard Kingsnorth for p.C9 (top), /Andy Caulfield for p.C9 (bottom), /Chris Ladd for p.C14 (top), /Daniel Pangbourne for p.C14 (centre), /Justin Pumfrey for p.C14 (bottom), /VCL/Alistair Berg for p.C15 (top right); Sally & Richard Greenhill Photo Library/Sally Greenhill for p.C1 (top), /Richard Greenhill for pp.C6 (bottom right), C16 (bottom); Robert Harding Picture Library/Dr Müller for p.C12 (top); Life File Photographic Library/Emma Lee for p.C6 (bottom left), /Angela Maynard for p.C15 (bottom right); W Lloyd Jerome for p.84; The Merrion Hotel, Dublin for p.58; Pictures Colour Library for p.C4 (top), p.C4 (bottom), and p.C7 (bottom); Sporting Pictures (UK)/Jardine for p.C6 (top right); <http://www.shoutpictures.com/>www.shoutpictures.com for p.C15 (top left).

Artwork: Oxford Designers & Illustrators

Picture research by Valerie Mulcahy

Text permissions by Jean Kennedy

Design concept by Peter Ducker

Cover design by Dunne & Scully

The recordings which accompany this book were made at Studio AVP, London

To *the student*

This book is for candidates preparing for the University of Cambridge ESOL Examinations First Certificate in English (FCE). The FCE examination is widely recognised in commerce and industry and in individual university faculties and other educational institutions.

The collection of four complete practice tests comprises past papers from the Cambridge First Certificate in English examination; you can practise these tests on your own or with the help of your teacher.

The FCE examination is part of a group of examinations developed by Cambridge ESOL called the Cambridge Main Suite. The Main Suite consists of five examinations that have similar characteristics but are designed for different levels of English language ability. Within the five levels, FCE is at Cambridge/ALTE Level 3, Level B2 in the Council of Europe Framework and Level 1 in the UK National Qualifications Framework.

Examination	Cambridge/ALTE Level	Council of Europe Framework Level	UK National Qualifications Framework Level
CPE Certificate of Proficiency in English	Level 5	C2	3
CAE Certificate in Advanced English	Level 4	C1	2
FCE First Certificate in English	Level 3	B2	1
PET Preliminary English Test	Level 2	B1	Entry 3
KET Key English Test	Level 1	A2	Entry 2
YLE Cambridge Young Learners English	Breakthrough Level		

The FCE examination consists of five papers:

Paper 1	**Reading**	1 hour 15 minutes
Paper 2	**Writing**	1 hour 30 minutes
Paper 3	**Use of English**	1 hour 15 minutes
Paper 4	**Listening**	40 minutes (approximately)
Paper 5	**Speaking**	14 minutes

Paper 1   Reading

This paper consists of **four parts**. Each part contains a text and some questions. Part 4 may contain two or more shorter related texts. There are **35 questions** in total, including multiple choice, gapped text and matching questions.

Paper 2   Writing

This paper consists of **two parts**. For both parts you have to write between 120 and 180 words. Part 1 is **compulsory**. It provides texts which are sometimes accompanied by visual material to help you write a letter.

In Part 2, there are four tasks from which you **choose one** to write about. The range of tasks from which questions may be drawn includes an article, a report, a composition, a short story and a letter. The last question is based on the set books. These books remain on the list for about two years and you should contact Cambridge ESOL, or the Cambridge ESOL Local Secretary in your area, if you wish to have the up-to-date list of set books. If you decide to do the question on the set books, there will be two options from which you can **choose one** to write about.

Paper 3   Use of English

This paper consists of **five parts** and tests your control of English grammar, vocabulary and spelling. There are **65 questions** in total. The tasks include gap-filling exercises, sentence transformation, word formation and error correction.

Paper 4   Listening

This paper contains **four parts**. Each part contains a recorded text or texts and some questions including multiple choice, note-taking, sentence completion and matching. You hear each text twice. There is a total of **30 questions**.

You will need to pause your audio CD before Parts 2, 3 and 4, and at the end of the test. The length of the pauses is announced to you. The audio cassettes, however, contain all pauses between parts, and only need to be paused for five minutes at the end of the test.

Paper 5   Speaking

This paper consists of **four parts**. The standard test format is two candidates and two examiners. One examiner takes part in the conversation, the other examiner listens and gives marks. You will be given photographs and other visual material to look at and talk about. Sometimes you will talk with the other candidate, sometimes with the examiner and sometimes with both.

Marks and results

Your overall FCE grade is based on the total score gained in all five papers. It is not necessary to achieve a satisfactory level in all five papers in order to pass the examination. Certificates are given to candidates who pass the examination with grade A, B or C. A is the highest. The minimum successful performance in order to achieve a grade C corresponds to about 60% of the total marks. D and E are failing grades. Your Statement of Results will include a graphical profile of your performance in each paper and show your relative performance in each one. Each paper is weighted to 40 marks. Therefore, the five FCE papers total 200 marks, after weighting.

Further information

For more information about FCE or any other Cambridge ESOL examination write to:

University of Cambridge
ESOL Examinations
1 Hills Road
Cambridge
CB1 2EU
England

Telephone: +44 1223 553355
Fax: +44 1223 460278
e-mail: ESOLHelpdesk@ucles.org.uk
www.CambridgeESOL.org

In some areas this information can also be obtained from the British Council.

Test 1

PAPER 1 READING (1 hour 15 minutes)

Part 1

You are going to read a magazine article about personal watercraft – also known as 'jet-skis'. Choose from the list **A-I** the sentence which best summarises each part (**1-7**) of the article. There is one extra sentence which you do not need to use. There is an example at the beginning (**0**).

Mark your answers **on the separate answer sheet**.

A Personal watercraft are now regarded as having a more serious role.

B There is now greater emphasis on the correct way of using personal watercraft.

C Personal watercraft are likely to grow in popularity in the future.

D Personal watercraft have changed because the kind of people using them has changed.

E The majority of people using personal watercraft do so because it is enjoyable.

F Personal watercraft used to have a terrible reputation.

G Personal watercraft enable you to experience travelling on the sea in relative comfort.

H The reason why people like using personal watercraft has changed.

I Personal watercraft enable you to combine opposing wishes.

First Certificate English 6
(CUP) ISBN: 0-521-78665-3

SPEEDING OVER SEAS

Jennai Cox reports on riding the ocean waves on personal watercraft.

| **0** | **I** |

If you like the water but are not keen on getting wet; if you enjoy speed but without the associated risks; if you like to keep active but prefer not to make too much effort; and if you have given up all hope of finding a sport that will accommodate your conflicting preferences, think again. Think personal watercraft.

| **1** | |

When the sport rose to popularity in Britain a few years ago, it was, like many thrilling new activities, taken up by young risk-takers. It became known as jet-skiing and before long was given a very bad name. The noise, the antics and, inevitably, the accidents caused by this unregulated sport annoyed anglers, sailors and swimmers alike.

| **2** | |

Having exhausted the number of thrills they could get from their personal watercraft, many of the younger sensation-seekers are moving on to more challenging activities. Left to the more mature in mind and years, the sport has been forced to grow up. Now that the average age of those purchasing personal watercraft is 42, and a growing percentage of the market is made up of families, the machines have had to adapt: two- and three-seater personal watercraft are becoming the norm.

| **3** | |

Mindful of past criticism, personal watercraft manufacturers are trying to ensure that all owners, especially the new ones, are taught seamanship, navigation and harbour rules. The machines are now registered and should be sold with a safety handbook and video, as well as an operator's guide.

| **4** | |

As with so many other powerful machines, it is not the vehicle that causes danger but the person driving it. But now that personal watercraft are becoming larger, more sophisticated and able to hold more fuel, the attraction has changed from danger to distance. More and more personal watercraft users today want to cruise.

| **5** | |

Riding on personal watercraft is like taking a civilised rollercoaster ride on water. Because you are so close to the elements, you feel more a part of them, without having to put up with their more unpleasant aspects. Apart from the odd splash, and wet feet, you stay comparatively dry and are much more able to enjoy the delights of being at sea.

| **6** | |

Having overcome hostility, personal watercraft and their users are gradually being seen in a more positive light. Despite being rich people's toys – they can cost several thousand pounds – their capabilities as lifeboat vehicles are beginning to be developed. Quick and easy to launch, they can reach swimmers who are in trouble or the shipwrecked very swiftly and, being so easy to manoeuvre, can be driven closer than many boats. A stretcher which can be pulled behind has also recently been developed.

| **7** | |

To drive personal watercraft safely at speed requires skill, agility, endurance and arm strength. But the basics are easy. The disabled have discovered that personal watercraft allow them to take part in a sport without feeling at a disadvantage. And for most people discovering personal watercraft, pursuing a competitive or fitness-improving activity is not the idea. Pleasure is the goal and most of them achieve it.

Part 2

You are going to read an extract from a novel. For questions **8-14**, choose the answer
(**A**, **B**, **C** or **D**) which you think fits best according to the text.

Mark your answers **on the separate answer sheet**.

Many trees in the Brackham area were brought down in the terrible storms that March. The town itself lost two great lime trees from the former market square. The disappearance of such prominent features had altered the appearance of the town centre entirely, to the annoyance of its more conservative inhabitants.

Among the annoyed, under more normal circumstances, would have been Chief Inspector Douglas Pelham, head of the local police force. But at the height of that week's storm, when the wind brought down even the mature walnut tree in his garden, Pelham had in fact been in no fit state to notice. A large and healthy man, he had for the first time in his life been seriously ill with an attack of bronchitis.

When he first complained of an aching head and tightness in his chest, his wife, Molly, had tried to persuade him to go to the doctor. Convinced that the police force could not do without him, he had, as usual, ignored her and attempted to carry on working. Predictably, though he wouldn't have listened to anyone who tried to tell him so, this had the effect of fogging his memory and shortening his temper.

It was only when his colleague, Sergeant Lloyd, took the initiative and drove him to the doctor's door that he finally gave in. By that time, he didn't have the strength left to argue with her. In no time at all, she was taking him along to the chemist's to get his prescribed antibiotics and then home to his unsurprised wife who sent him straight to bed.

When Molly told him, on the Thursday morning, that the walnut tree had been brought down during the night, Pelham hadn't been able to take it in. On Thursday evening, he had asked weakly about damage to the house, groaned thankfully when he heard there was none, and pulled the sheets over his head.

It wasn't until Saturday, when the antibiotics took effect, his temperature dropped and he got up, that he realised with a shock that the loss of the walnut tree had made a permanent difference to the appearance of the living-room. The Pelhams' large house stood in a sizeable garden. It had not come cheap, but even so Pelham had no regrets about buying it. The leafy garden had created an impression of privacy. Now, though, the storm had changed his outlook. Previously the view from the living-room had featured the handsome walnut tree. This had not darkened the room because there was also a window on the opposite wall, but it had provided interesting patterns of light and shade that disguised the true state of the worn furniture that the family had brought with them from their previous house.

With the tree gone, the room seemed cruelly bright, its worn furnishings exposed in all their shabbiness. And the view from the window didn't bear looking at. The tall house next door, previously hidden by the tree, was now there, dominating the outlook with its unattractive purple bricks and external pipes. It seemed to have a great many upstairs windows, all of them watching the Pelhams' every movement.

'Doesn't it look terrible?' Pelham croaked to his wife.

But Molly, standing in the doorway, sounded more pleased than dismayed. 'That's what I've been telling you ever since we came here. We have to buy a new sofa, whatever it costs.'

4

8   Why were some people in Brackham annoyed after the storm?

    A   The town looked different.
    B   The police had done little to help.
    C   No market could be held.
    D   Fallen trees had not been removed.

9   Who does 'her' in line 17 refer to?

    A   Molly Pelham
    B   the doctor
    C   Sergeant Lloyd
    D   the chemist

10   When Chief Inspector Pelham's wife first told him about the walnut tree, he appeared to be

    A   worried.
    B   shocked.
    C   saddened.
    D   uninterested.

11   What aspect of the Pelhams' furniture does 'shabbiness' in line 33 describe?

    A   its colour
    B   its condition
    C   its position
    D   its design

12   As a result of the storm, the Pelhams' living-room

    A   was pleasantly lighter.
    B   felt less private.
    C   had a better view.
    D   was in need of repair.

13   Why did Molly sound pleased by her husband's comment?

    A   It proved that he was well again.
    B   She agreed about the tree.
    C   She thought he meant the sofa.
    D   It was what she expected him to say.

14   From what we learn of Chief Inspector Pelham, he could best be described as

    A   open-minded.
    B   well-liked.
    C   warm-hearted.
    D   strong-willed.

Part 3

You are going to read a magazine article about country music star Pam Tillis. Eight paragraphs have been removed from the article. Choose from the paragraphs **A-I** the one which fits each gap (**15-21**). There is one extra paragraph which you do not need to use. There is an example at the beginning (**0**).

Mark your answers **on the separate answer sheet**.

Wild Angel

Country music star Pam Tillis talks about her life and work.

While in the studio recording her album *All Of This Love*, country music star Pam Tillis found herself imagining an old dance hall. As a result, the Mexican-flavoured ballad, 'Tequila Mockingbird', one of the album's highlights, is punctuated by the sound of her dance steps.

0	I

The eldest child of famed country singer Mel Tillis, Pam has been in the business long enough to know when to add something a little unusual to her music. But far from being the 'golden child' with a one-way ticket to success, Pam Tillis's journey to stardom has been full of ups and downs.

15	

Then her life was turned upside down. At the age of 16, Pam was involved in a serious car accident, leading to years of plastic surgery and occasional pain ever since.

16	

After the accident, she attended the University of Tennessee, and it was here that Pam started her first band. Leaving college in 1976, she worked for a time in her father's publishing company, Sawgrass Music, but then it was time to leave the nest.

17	

In the late 1970s, this area was a magnet for young Americans. There was no better place to be, and Pam's new friends there encouraged her to widen her musical tastes.

18	

'It was a crazy time,' Pam recalls. 'When you're young, you go any way the wind blows, so I was experimenting and seeing what I could do. I was searching for my identity, if you like.'

19	

Returning to Nashville in 1978, Pam was still looking for her place. Some of her songs had been recorded by other artists, but she now began the search for her first recording contract.

20	

The rest, as they say, is history. Recently voted Female Singer of the Year by the Country Music Association, and with a series of best-selling records behind her, the most difficult part of Pam's life these days is balancing her home life, with her husband and young son, and her career.

21	

'In some ways it was worse in Dad's day,' admits Pam. 'There was no TV or video and they were away 100 days or more a year. But the sacrifice is worth it. It's a way of teaching your kids about having a dream, and how important it is to follow that dream.'

A However, this took longer than she expected, and having a famous father didn't automatically open doors. She sang in a rhythm and blues band, and after five years of writing and singing, finally got her big chance.

B Pam enjoyed playing with the group she had formed. 'There's enormous energy out there,' she states emphatically. 'I lasted just over a year, but then it was time to go home.'

C Pam first appeared on a major stage at the age of eight, singing with her father. As a teenager, she showed up at many talent nights in Nashville, and performed at local clubs.

D Pam, however, produced her latest record herself. 'It was rewarding and enjoyable,' she says, 'but I wish I'd been able to take a whole year over it.'

E California has always been the destination for America's hopefuls and dreamers. Pam felt limited by life in Nashville, and so she too moved to the west coast.

F However, having the advantage of growing up in the music business herself, Pam knows what this involves. She understands what is necessary in terms of hard work and lonely nights spent in hotel rooms.

G Pam believes that the experience gave her a greater determination to live the life she wanted. 'If something dramatic like that happens to anyone, it makes them think they survived for a reason.'

H One in particular told her that she was capable of singing any kind of music she wanted. Keen to spread her artistic wings, she put together a 'loose jazz/rock band' called Freelight.

I 'It wasn't planned. My violin player started to play his solo and my mind was transported to a time about 200 years ago. When I started dancing, the noise seemed so appropriate that we left it on the record.'

Part 4

You are going to read a magazine article about five young designers. For questions **22-35**, choose from the designers (**A-E**). The designers may be chosen more than once. When more than one answer is required, these may be given in any order. There is an example at the beginning (**0**).

Mark your answers **on the separate answer sheet**.

Which designer(s)

works in a variety of environments?	**0** C	
advises against certain styles?	**22**	
says they took a business decision based on their own personal taste?	**23**	
had begun designing before being trained?	**24**	
have adapted a traditional style?	**25**	**26**
is working with a material which is new to them?	**27**	
have used their reputation to develop a new area of business?	**28**	**29**
are completely self-taught?	**30**	**31**
mention how tastes have changed recently?	**32**	**33**
have received professional recognition?	**34**	**35**

Style Merchants

Style informs every part of our lives today from clothes to interior decoration and accessories. Jo Foley provides a taste of the trends for this year's followers of fashion.

A Ned Ingham: Dress Designer

Ned Ingham makes dreamy, romantic wedding dresses. 'People are turning away from the traditional, rather stiff dresses to much simpler styles,' he explains. Ingham has been drawing and designing wedding dresses since he was a schoolboy. Then, at the age of 16, he enrolled at fashion school, where he gained the technical skills to cut and construct clothes. But you do not have to be a bride to own an Ingham dress: he also designs long, classic evening dresses, given a fresh touch by up-to-the-minute colours and fabrics. For the less adventurous, Ingham's designs include a classical summer navy-blue suit, the centrepiece of the Englishwoman's wardrobe for most of the 20th century. But in his hands, it looks as new as tomorrow.

B Sally Quail: Jeweller

Although she once worked for an art dealer, Sally Quail has had no formal training in jewellery. It was only when she could not find an engagement ring she liked that she decided to design her own. The resulting enquiries encouraged her to set up as a designer in 1990. Now her pieces are sought out by many stars of stage and screen. Her signature style is large semi-precious stones set in gold to make magnificent necklaces, bracelets and rings fashioned after those worn in the 18th century. However, she has recently begun to use the most precious stone of all – diamonds. 'It must reflect my age,' says 36-year-old Quail. 'I reached that moment in every woman's life when she wants a diamond and that is when I began working with them.'

C Penny Pratt: Florist

In addition to running her tiny shop, Penny Pratt is a flower consultant for a large chain of supermarkets and provides floral ideas to a number of top restaurants. All of this is good going for someone who has no floristry qualifications and gave up her job as a teacher 10 years ago in order to do 'something different'. And her simple, yet incredibly modern, creations have begun to capture every design prize in the flower business, which has helped her in setting up her own London Flower School. She has recently combined her skills on extremely successful lecture trips to Japan and the USA. She says, 'Flower arrangements are much simpler these days. Keep them simple but strong and don't have too many leaves – they are too large and architectural. For wedding bouquets, whatever your arrangement, the golden rule remains the flowers must be of the same species.'

D Peter Little: Hairdresser

For over 20 years, Peter Little has taken his scissors to some of the world's top heads. Everyone who is anyone has had their hair styled by this man. 'Most women want real-looking hair and a style they can manage at home,' he says. So his approach is a novel one – to ensure that his clients never appear as if they have just walked out of a salon. But this carefree attitude and casual look does not come cheap – £250 for the first appointment, and there's a three-month waiting list. Trading on his celebrity, Peter has produced his own range of hairdryers and other styling equipment. Now, those who can't make it to his salon can create their own styles back at home.

E Lily Grimson: Handbag Designer

Just four years after setting up in the fiercely competitive fashion business, Lily Grimson, with only an introductory course in art and design behind her, has had two of her creations selected for a major design exhibition. Whatever the shape and form of her designs, they are never ignored. All of Grimson's fashion bags are handmade in the UK. The Grimson handbag is not simply a container – the bags are full of glamour, whether fashioned from the finest calfskin or the heaviest silk. A combination of chic and care make a Grimson bag something special.

PAPER 2   WRITING (1 hour 30 minutes)

Part 1

You **must** answer this question.

1   You ordered a gift by post for a friend's birthday. The company were late sending the gift to you and you were also not happy with it. Below is the advertisement for the gift, on which you have written some notes.

Read the advertisement, together with your notes. Then, using all the information in your notes, write a **letter** to Mr P. Marsden of Personal Pens Limited. You should explain why you are not happy with the gift and ask for your money back.

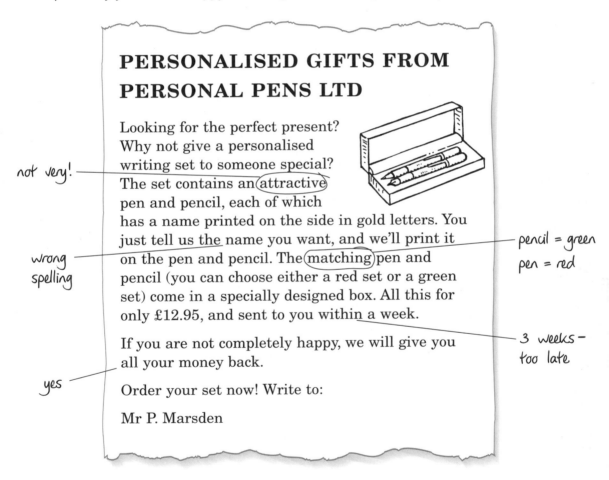

PERSONALISED GIFTS FROM PERSONAL PENS LTD

not very!

Looking for the perfect present? Why not give a personalised writing set to someone special? The set contains an (attractive) pen and pencil, each of which has a name printed on the side in gold letters. You just tell us the name you want, and we'll print it on the pen and pencil. The (matching) pen and pencil (you can choose either a red set or a green set) come in a specially designed box. All this for only £12.95, and sent to you within a week.

wrong spelling

pencil = green
pen = red

3 weeks – too late

If you are not completely happy, we will give you all your money back.

yes

Order your set now! Write to:

Mr P. Marsden

Write a **letter** of between **120** and **180** words in an appropriate style on the opposite page. Do not write any postal addresses.

Question 1

....
....
....
....
....
....
....
....
....
....
....
....
....
....
....
....
....
....
....
....
....
....
....
....
....
....
....
....
....

Part 2

Write an answer to **one** of the questions **2-5** in this part. Write your answer in **120-180** words in an appropriate style on the opposite page. Put the question number in the box.

2   You have had a class discussion on fashion. Your teacher has now asked you to write a composition, giving your opinions on the following statement:

Young people always want to dress differently from their parents.

Write your **composition**.

3   You see this announcement in your school magazine.

> ## *New Clubs after School*
>
> *Your school wants to start some new after-school clubs. Chess, table tennis, guitar playing and cookery have been suggested as possible ideas for clubs. What do you think? Write us an article for the school magazine covering the points below.*
>
> - *Tell us which **one** of these four ideas you like best **and** why.*
> - *Make **one** other suggestion for a new club **and** explain why it would be a good idea.*

Write your **article**.

4   The local tourist office has asked you to write a report on interesting things for visitors to see and do on a **one-day** sightseeing tour of your area. In your report, include suggestions about where visitors should go and what they should do in order to spend an interesting day in your area.

Write your **report**.

5   Answer **one** of the following two questions based on your reading of **one** of these set books. Write (**a**) or (**b**) as well as the number **5** in the question box, and the **title** of the book next to the box. Your answer **must** be about one of the books below.

Best Detective Stories of Agatha Christie – Longman Fiction
The Old Man and the Sea – Ernest Hemingway
A Window on the Universe – Oxford Bookworms Collection
Cry Freedom – John Briley
Wuthering Heights – Emily Brontë

Either   (**a**)   You have had a class discussion on whether the characters in the book or short story you have read are believable. Your teacher has now asked you to write a composition on this subject. Write your **composition**, explaining your views with reference to the book or one of the short stories you have read.

Or   (**b**)   An English-speaking friend is going on a long journey soon and has asked you to recommend a book to read during the journey. Write a **letter** to your friend, giving some information about the book or short stories you have read. You should give reasons for your recommendation.

Question |

....
....
....
....
....
....
....
....
....
....
....
....
....
....
....
....
....
....
....
....
....
....
....
....
....
....
....
....
....
....
....

PAPER 3   USE OF ENGLISH (1 hour 15 minutes)

Part 1

For questions **1-15**, read the text below and decide which answer (**A**, **B**, **C** or **D**) best fits each space. There is an example at the beginning (**0**).

Mark your answers **on the separate answer sheet**.

Example:

0	**A** learn	**B** capture	**C** discover	**D** get

0	A	B	C	D
	—	—	—	—

LEARNING TO MAKE A PERFECT PIZZA

According to the European Pizza-Makers' Association, making a good pizza is not a straightforward skill to **(0)** ..... . The ingredients seem very **(1)** ..... : flour, yeast, water and a bit of salt. But water and flour can easily **(2)** ..... glue and anyone who has eaten a **(3)** ..... quality pizza will know how bad it can make your stomach **(4)** ..... .

'In Italy, 70 per cent of pizza makers could improve on their product, not to **(5)** ..... all the pizza makers around the world who **(6)** ..... uneatable meals,' says Antonio Primiceri, the Association's founder. He has now started a pizza school in an attempt to **(7)** ..... the reputation of this traditional dish. As part of an **(8)** ..... course, the students at Mr Primiceri's school are taught to **(9)** ..... common mistakes, produce a good basic mixture, add a tasty topping and cook the pizza properly. 'Test the finished pizza by breaking the crust,' advises Mr Primiceri. 'If the soft **(10)** ..... inside the pizza is white, clean and dry, it's a good pizza. If it is not like this, the pizza will **(11)** ..... your stomach. You will feel **(12)** ..... full and also thirsty.'

In Italy alone, the pizza **(13)** ..... has an annual turnover of more than $12 billion. Mr Primiceri **(14)** ..... that there are 10,000 jobs in pizza restaurants waiting to be **(15)** ..... by those with real skill. 'If you are a good pizza cook, you will never be without a job,' he says.

1 **A** simple   **B** primary   **C** pure   **D** regular

2 **A** mix   **B** construct   **C** assemble   **D** make

3 **A** sad   **B** poor   **C** short   **D** weak

4 **A** sense   **B** do   **C** feel   **D** be

5 **A** state   **B** mention   **C** remark   **D** tell

6 **A** submit   **B** give   **C** serve   **D** deal

7 **A** save   **B** provide   **C** deliver   **D** return

8 **A** extensive   **B** extreme   **C** intensive   **D** intentional

9 **A** pass   **B** escape   **C** miss   **D** avoid

10 **A** spot   **B** part   **C** side   **D** slice

11 **A** worry   **B** upset   **C** ache   **D** depress

12 **A** hardly   **B** tightly   **C** uncomfortably **D** heavily

13 **A** activity   **B** body   **C** industry   **D** company

14 **A** computes   **B** estimates   **C** assesses   **D** counts

15 **A** employed   **B** filled   **C** completed   **D** covered

Part 2

For questions **16-30**, read the text below and think of the word which best fits each space. Use only **one** word in each space. There is an example at the beginning (**0**). Write your answers **on the separate answer sheet**.

Example: | **0** | *it* |

HOLLYWOOD

How was (**0**) ....*it*.... that Hollywood came to be the place everyone associates with the American film industry? It's a strange story.

There was a little village in southern California called Cahuenga Valley (**16**) .... a Mr and Mrs Wilcox had their home. In 1887, (**17**) .... Mrs Wilcox was on a trip to the east coast, she got into conversation (**18**) .... a stranger on a train. The stranger had a home called Hollywood somewhere else in the country, (**19**) .... Mrs Wilcox liked the name (**20**) .... much that she decided to give her home the same name. Because the Wilcox's home was the biggest in Cahuenga Valley, the village soon became known (**21**) .... Hollywood.

In normal circumstances most people (**22**) .... never have heard of Hollywood. However, between 1908 and 1913 (**23**) .... else happened. Many small independent film companies began moving to southern California (**24**) .... two main reasons. Firstly, they were attracted by the sunny climate, which let them film throughout the year (**25**) .... the need for expensive lighting. Secondly, they were (**26**) .... problems with the larger, more powerful studios in New York, and they wanted to get away from there.

Only one studio actually set (**27**) .... in Hollywood. Local people were so angry when it appeared that (**28**) .... law was passed forbidding the building of any more studios. In fact, Hollywood itself never had a film industry, surprisingly enough, (**29**) .... the other studios that came to the area were all built outside Hollywood. Nevertheless, by 1915 'Hollywood' (**30**) .... become familiar as a term for the movie business as a whole.

Part 3

For questions **31-40**, complete the second sentence so that it has a similar meaning to the first sentence, using the word given. **Do not change the word given**. You must use between **two** and **five** words, including the word given.

Here is an example (**0**).

Example:

0   You must do exactly what the manager tells you.

carry

You must ……………………….........…………. instructions exactly.

The gap can be filled by the words 'carry out the manager's' so you write:

0	*carry out the manager's*

Write **only the missing words** on the separate answer sheet.

---

31   So that John could go on holiday in the summer, he saved £10 a week.

order

John saved £10 a week .... able to go on holiday in the summer.

32   It's not worth asking the manager for the day off.

point

There .... in asking the manager for the day off.

33   We had to finish all the work before we could leave.

until

We had to stay .... all the work.

34   Tim had not expected the concert to be so good.

better

The concert .... had expected.

35 If Cheryl doesn't train harder, she'll never get into the swimming team.

does

Cheryl will never get into the swimming team ....
more training.

36 'Do you realise what the time is, Steve?' asked Chris.

what

Chris asked Steve .... it was.

37 The company decided to advertise the job in a national newspaper.

put

The company decided to .... the job in a
national newspaper.

38 At the end of his speech, the winner thanked his parents.

finished

The winner .... his parents.

39 I applied for the job a month ago.

month

It .... I applied for the job.

40 They received many letters of support after they had appeared on television.

following

They received many letters of support ....
on television.

Part 4

For questions **41-55**, read the text below and look carefully at each line. Some of the lines are correct, and some have a word which should not be there.

If a line is correct, put a tick (✓) by the number **on the separate answer sheet**. If a line has a word which should **not** be there, write the word **on the separate answer sheet**. There are two examples at the beginning (**0** and **00**).

Examples:

0	✓
00	*me*

TAKING BETTER PHOTOGRAPHS

0	Like many people, I have had a camera for almost as long as I can
00	remember, and I have always enjoyed me taking photographs of
41	my family and friends, and places I have been visited. Then, about a year
42	ago, I noticed that most of the photos I was so proud of which were in
43	fact all very similar to each other. They all showed groups of people
44	standing by a famous building or some other attraction. You hardly
45	couldn't make out their faces clearly, and so it was difficult to get
46	an idea of how had everybody felt. I was looking for a new hobby at
47	the time, and have decided that I would start taking photography
48	more seriously. I thought it would be expensive, but, after reading
49	a few chapters of a book I borrowed from a friend, I last realised that
50	I could improve a great deal extra without spending a lot of money on new
51	equipment. Soon, instead of just taking out the same old pictures, I
52	was photographing those trees, animals, people I didn't know and so
53	on. This soon made a real difference to the quality of my photographs
54	as I began to concentrate myself on getting the best picture possible. I
55	am pleased with the results because I have achieved in such a short time.

Part 5

For questions **56-65**, read the text below. Use the word given in capitals at the end of each line to form a word that fits in the space in the same line. There is an example at the beginning (**0**). Write your answers **on the separate answer sheet**.

Example: | **0** | *meeting* |

A NEW SUPERMARKET FOR THE TOWN

At a **(0)** ...*meeting*. held in Oxwell last Thursday evening a wide	**MEET**
(56) ..... of opinions was expressed on plans to build a large	**VARY**
supermarket in the town. A **(57)** ..... of the supermarket group	**DIRECT**
stated that the supermarket would benefit the **(58)** ..... of	**INHABIT**
Oxwell as it would give people more **(59)** ..... when shopping	**CHOOSE**
and would lead to a **(60)** ..... in the number of jobs available in	**GROW**
the town, which has a high rate of **(61)** ..... . Although there was	**EMPLOY**
(62) ..... on the need for new jobs, some of those present	**AGREE**
claimed that the supermarket would lead to a **(63)** ..... of jobs as	**LOSE**
small shops, **(64)** ..... to compete with supermarket prices,	**ABLE**
would be forced to close. The final **(65)** ..... on whether or	**DECIDE**
not to build the supermarket will be made next month.	

PAPER 4   LISTENING (approximately 40 minutes)

Part 1

You will hear people talking in eight different situations. For questions **1-8**, choose the best answer (**A**, **B** or **C**).

---

1 You hear part of a radio play.
Where is the scene taking place?

A   in the street

B   in a bank

C   in a police station

| 1 |

2 You overhear the beginning of a lecture.
What subject are the students taking?

A   medicine

B   sport

C   music

| 2 |

3 You overhear a conversation in a college.
Who is the young man?

A   a new student

B   a student in the middle of a course

C   a former student

| 3 |

4 You hear a woman on the radio talking about a cookbook.
What does she regret?

A   not looking after it

B   not having kept it

C   not using it properly

| 4 |

First Certificate English 6 (CUP)
ISBN: 0-521-75445-3

5 You hear someone talking about the day he met someone famous.
How did he feel after meeting Chris Turner?

    A   unimpressed with the footballer

    B   angry with his friend

    C   disappointed with himself

                                                     5

6 You hear a woman talking on the phone.
Why has she called?

    A   to request a meeting

    B   to offer assistance

    C   to apologise for her absence

                                                     6

7 You overhear an extract from a radio play.
What is the young woman's relationship with the man?

    A   She's a pupil of his.

    B   She's a relative of his.

    C   She's a patient of his.

                                                     7

8 You hear someone telling a story about a strange thing that
happened in the mountains.
What point does the story prove?

    A   how strange things can be explained simply

    B   how easy it is to imagine things

    C   how you can be tricked by the silence

                                                     8

Part 2

You will hear part of a talk about dolls. For questions **9-18**, complete the sentences.

The first known dolls were found in [_____ **9**] in ancient Egypt.

The earliest dolls in the museum date from the [_____ **10**]

Early European dolls were dressed like [_____ **11**]

On the 17th-century dolls, you can see details like the [_____ **12**]

17th-century dolls may cost as much as [_____ **13**] each.

Collectors look for examples in perfect condition, with their [_____ **14**]

19th-century dolls had [_____ **15**] and real hair.

If you can take off the doll's hair, you may see the

[_____ **16**] underneath.

Before the 20th-century, all dolls were [_____ **17**] , not babies.

From the 1930s, dolls were made of [_____ **18**]

Part 3

You will hear five different people talking about why they decided to become nurses. For questions **19-23**, choose which of the reasons (**A-F**) each speaker is giving. Use the letters only once. There is one extra letter which you do not need to use.

A It was a childhood dream.

Speaker 1 | **19**

B Teachers had recommended it.

Speaker 2 | **20**

C A friend had decided to do it.

Speaker 3 | **21**

D It offered a secure income.

Speaker 4 | **22**

E It is a family tradition.

Speaker 5 | **23**

F It is emotionally satisfying.

Part 4

You will hear part of a radio programme in which a book critic gives information about three new books on the subject of travelling in the United States of America. For questions **24-30**, decide which book each statement refers to. Write **A** for **A to Z**,

J for **Just Go** or

TT for **Travel Treat**.

---

24 It gives information about political developments.

| | 24 |

25 It has been carefully researched.

| | 25 |

26 It is excellent on the subject of less well-known places.

| | 26 |

27 It aims to be amusing but fails.

| | 27 |

28 It gives the best advice on health.

| | 28 |

29 It helps the traveller to save money.

| | 29 |

30 It gives advice on accommodation for all budgets.

| | 30 |

PAPER 5　SPEAKING　(14 minutes)

You take the Speaking test with another candidate, referred to here as your partner. There are two examiners. One will speak to you and your partner and the other will be listening. Both examiners will award marks.

Part 1 (3 minutes)

The examiner asks you and your partner questions about yourselves. You may be asked about things like 'your home town', 'your interests', 'your career plans', etc.

Part 2 (4 minutes)

The examiner gives you two photographs and asks you to talk about them for one minute. The examiner then asks your partner a question about your photographs and your partner responds briefly.

Then the examiner gives your partner two different photographs. Your partner talks about these photographs for one minute. This time the examiner asks you a question about your partner's photographs and you respond briefly.

Part 3 (approximately 3 minutes)

The examiner asks you and your partner to talk together. You may be asked to solve a problem or try to come to a decision about something. For example, you might be asked to decide the best way to use some rooms in a language school. The examiner gives you a picture to help you but does not join in the conversation.

Part 4 (approximately 4 minutes)

The examiner joins in the conversation. You all talk together in a more general way about what has been said in Part 3. The examiner asks you questions but you and your partner are also expected to develop the conversation.

Test 2

PAPER 1   READING (1 hour 15 minutes)

Part 1

You are going to read an article about research into yawning. Choose from the list **A-I** the most suitable heading for each part (**1-7**) of the article. There is one extra heading which you do not need to use. There is an example at the beginning (**0**).

Mark your answers **on the separate answer sheet**.

A   An aid to achievement

B   Failure to prove a theory

C   A way to send people to sleep

D   Losing the battle

E   Questioning a widespread belief

F   Results which support a theory

G   Not widely researched

H   A partly explained theory

I   Behaviour that spreads quickly

Yawning

0 | I

When one person yawns in a room, other people begin to yawn. Yawning is contagious, and once you start, there is almost nothing you can do to stop. Of course, the big question is: why do we yawn at all? What possible advantage can there be in keeping our mouths wide open for several seconds? Is it a need for oxygen? Too much carbon dioxide in the blood? Time for bed?

1 |

It is none of these according to Robert Provine, an American psychologist. Provine first became curious about yawning when he realised that nobody had really studied this extremely common aspect of behaviour. 'Most scientists are looking for the deep and obscure,' Provine says. 'I look for the significance of everyday behaviour that people have neglected.' With this in mind, he and several other psychologists decided to find out when, why and how we yawn.

2 |

Conventional wisdom has long held that we yawn in order to wake up our weary brains with a refreshing burst of oxygen. Assuming that this is true, Provine reasoned, then people who are running low on oxygen – or high on carbon dioxide – should yawn more often than normal. To find out if this was the case, Provine first had to try to make people yawn more.

3 |

In his laboratory, Provine gathered together a group of students and told them to think about yawning while they breathed in mixtures of air that were either high in oxygen, high in carbon dioxide or completely normal. Although the gases made the students breathe faster, none of the different gases altered the students' rate of yawning, which held steady at about 24 yawns an hour. Exercise, which also speeds up breathing, made no difference to the yawning rate either.

4 |

Whatever the reason for yawning, there is no doubt that it is refreshing. According to Ronald Baenninger, another psychologist who is interested in the subject, this feeling is not caused by oxygen coming into the body. The cause, he believes, may lie in the blood: yawning sends an extra supply of blood to the brain. We do not know exactly what the blood does when it reaches the brain, but Baenninger believes it does help to refresh it.

5 |

Baenninger believes, therefore, that we yawn in order to make our brains ready for some new action. To test this theory, he asked people to wear bands around their wrists as they went about their normal routines. These bands were sensitive to increased movement by the people wearing them. The bands contained a button which the people were told to press every time they yawned. After collecting data for two weeks, Baenninger found that within 15 minutes of yawning his subjects were normally engaged in some more lively form of activity.

6 |

There are indeed plenty of indications from everyday life to suggest that yawning helps the brain to get ready for something big. Olympic athletes yawn before a race, students yawn before an examination, and violinists yawn before a concert. It is not that the athletes, students or violinists are bored; they are simply working to get to a level at which they are well and truly ready for the main event.

7 |

'We yawn when there is nothing actually happening but when we do not want to lose our level of readiness,' says Baenninger. Why we yawn before going to bed, though, remains a mystery. Baenninger suggests that it may be that we struggle to stay awake and alert, but sleep simply wins out in the end.

Part 2

You are going to read an extract from a novel. For questions **8-15**, choose the answer
(**A**, **B**, **C** or **D**) which you think fits best according to the text.

Mark your answers **on the separate answer sheet**.

On Saturday mornings I worked in the family shop. I started cycling down to the shop with Dad on Saturdays as soon as I was big enough. I thought of it as giving him a hand and so I didn't mind what I did, although it was mostly just fetching and carrying at a run all morning. I managed not to think of it as work and I looked forward to the bar of chocolate my grandmother passed me unsmilingly as I left. I tried not to look at her; I had reason to feel guilty because I'd generally already eaten some dried fruits or a sliver of cheese when no one was looking. As soon as I was fifteen, though, Dad said, 'That's it, our Janet. You're of working age now and you're not coming to work unless your grandmother pays you properly.' He did his best to make his chin look determined. 'I shall speak to her.'

The next Saturday, Gran called me into her little office behind the shop. I always hated going in there. She had an electric heater on full blast, and the windows were always kept tightly closed whatever the weather. 'You're wanting to get paid, I hear,' she said. 'Yes, please,' I replied. It was rather like visiting the headmistress at school, so I was very quiet and respectful. Gran searched through the mess of papers on her crowded desk, sighing and clicking her tongue. Eventually she produced an official-looking leaflet and ran her fingers along the columns of figures. 'How old are you?' 'Fifteen … Gran,' I added for extra politeness, but she looked at me as if I had been cheeky. 'Full-timers at your age get forty pounds for a thirty-five-hour week,' she announced in such a way as to leave no doubt that she wasn't in favour of this. 'No wonder there's no profit in shopkeeping! So, Janet, what's that per hour?'

Questions like that always flustered me. Instead of trying to work them out in my head, I would just stand there, unable to think straight. 'I'll get a pencil and paper,' I offered. 'Don't bother,' snapped Gran angrily, 'I'll do it myself. I'll give you a pound an hour; take it or leave it.' 'I'll take it, please.' 'And I expect real work for it, mind. No standing about, and if I catch you eating any of the stock, there'll be trouble. That's theft, and it's a crime.'

From then on, my main job at the shop was filling the shelves. This was dull, but I hardly expected to be trusted with handling the money. Once or twice, however, when Dad was extra busy, I'd tried to help him by serving behind the counter. I hated it. It was very difficult to remember the prices of everything and I was particularly hopeless at using the till. Certain customers made unkind remarks about this, increasing my confusion and the chances of my making a fool of myself.

It was an old-established village shop, going back 150 years at least and it was really behind the times even then. Dad longed to be able to make the shop more attractive to customers, but Gran wouldn't hear of it. I overheard them once arguing about whether to buy a freezer cabinet. 'Our customers want frozen food,' Dad said. 'They see things advertised and if they can't get them from us, they'll go elsewhere.' 'Your father always sold fresh food,' Gran replied. 'People come here for quality, they don't want all that frozen stuff.'

Actually, she gave way in the end over the freezer. Mr Timson, her great rival, installed one in his shop at the other end of the village and customers started making loud comments about how handy it was, being able to get frozen food in the village, and how good Mr Timson's sausages were. That really upset her because she was proud of her sausages and she ungraciously gave Dad the money to buy the freezer. Within a couple of weeks, she was eating frozen food like the rest of us.

8   How did Janet feel when she first started her Saturday morning job?

    A   She enjoyed the work that she was given.

    B   She was pleased to be helping her father.

    C   She worried that she was not doing it well.

    D   She was only really interested in the reward.

9   What do we learn about her grandmother's office in paragraph two?

    A   It needed decorating.

    B   It was untidy.

    C   It had too much furniture in it.

    D   It was dark.

10   'This' (line 18) refers to

    A   shopkeepers' profits.

    B   a thirty-five-hour week.

    C   Janet's request.

    D   the recommended wage.

11   'Flustered' (line 19) means

    A   bored.

    B   angered.

    C   confused.

    D   depressed.

12   Why did Janet's grandmother react angrily to her offer to fetch a pencil and paper?

    A   Janet was unable to answer her question.

    B   Janet had been unwilling to help her.

    C   Janet had made an unhelpful suggestion.

    D   Janet had answered her rudely.

13   What did Janet's father and grandmother disagree about?

    A   how to keep their customers loyal to the shop

    B   the type of advertising needed to attract customers

    C   the type of customers they needed to attract

    D   how to get new customers to come to the shop

14   What eventually persuaded Janet's grandmother to buy a freezer?

    A   She found that she liked frozen food after all.

    B   A new shop opening in the village had one.

    C   It was suggested that her products weren't fresh.

    D   She responded to pressure from her customers.

15   What impression do we get of Janet's feelings towards her grandmother?

    A   She respected her fairness.

    B   She doubted her judgement.

    C   She disliked her manner.

    D   She admired her determination.

Part 3

You are going to read an article written by someone who lives in a house in a valley. Seven sentences have been removed from the article. Choose from the sentences **A-H** the one which fits each gap (**16-21**). There is one extra sentence which you do not need to use. There is an example at the beginning (**0**).

Mark your answers **on the separate answer sheet**.

LIVING IN THE VALLEY

We had been living in our valley for sixteen months when we first realised the dangers that could exist. **0** **H** Until then, we had felt safe and sheltered in our valley.

Soon snow began to fall. Within a day it lay some 15 centimetres deep. **16** But on the neighbouring heights the snow was much deeper and stayed for longer. Up there the wind blasted fiercely. Deep in our valley we felt only sudden gusts of wind; trees swayed but the branches held firm.

And yet we knew that there was reason for us to worry. The snow and wind were certainly inconvenient but they did not really trouble us greatly. **17** It reminded us of what could have occurred if circumstances had been different, if the flow of water from the hills had not, many years before, been controlled, held back by a series of dams.

In a short time the snow started to melt. Day after day, we watched furious clouds pile up high over the hills to the west. Sinister grey clouds extended over the valleys. **18** We had seen enough of the sky; now we began to watch the river, which every day was becoming fuller and wilder.

The snow was gradually washed away as more and more rain streamed from the clouds, but high up in the hills the reservoir was filling and was fast approaching danger level. And then it happened – for the first time in years the reservoir overflowed. **19**

The river seemed maddened as the waters poured almost horizontally down to its lower stretches. Just a couple of metres from our cottage, the stream seemed wild beneath the bridge. **20**⬚ For three days we prayed that it would stay below its wall. Our prayers were answered as the dam held and the waters began to subside.

On many occasions through the centuries before the dam was built, the river had flooded the nearby villages in just such a rage. Now, though, the dam restricts the flow of the river and usually all is well; the great mass of water from the hills, the product of snow and torrential rain, remains behind its barrier with just the occasional overflow. **21**⬚ We can feel our home in the valley is still secure and safe.

A It was the river, the Ryburn, which normally flowed so gently, that threatened us most.

B And yet the immense power of all this water above us prevents us from ever believing ourselves to be completely safe in our home.

C They twisted and turned, rising eastwards and upwards, warning of what was to come.

D It was far deeper than we'd ever seen it so near our home, lunging furiously at its banks.

E We can thus enjoy, rather than fear, the huge clouds that hang over the valley, and can be thrilled by the tremendous power which we know the river possesses.

F It almost completely blocked our lane and made the streamside path slippery and dangerous.

G There in the heights it was like the Niagara Falls, as the water surged over the edge of the dam and poured into the stream below.

H It was the year when the storms came early, before the calendar even hinted at winter, even before November was out.

Part 4

You are going to read a magazine article in which five people talk about their characters. For questions **22-35**, choose from the people (**A-E**). The people may be chosen more than once. When more than one answer is required, these may be given in any order. There is an example at the beginning (**0**).

Mark your answers **on the separate answer sheet**.

Which person or people state(s) the following?

I used to avoid giving my opinions at work.	**0** E	
Taking time off for your professional development can make you feel more self-assured.	**22**	
I never thought I'd be a confident person.	**23**	
I'm not influenced by people's opinions of me.	**24**	
Everyone gets nervous at times.	**25**	**26**
Initially, I misunderstood what confidence was.	**27**	
I find making notes very supportive in my work.	**28**	
A certain event changed the course of my life.	**29**	**30**
I've worked on having a confident appearance.	**31**	
I am realistic about my abilities.	**32**	**33**
My behaviour helps others relax too.	**34**	
Getting things wrong can have a positive result.	**35**	

Confident people
What's their secret?

Confident people may look as though they were born that way, but most will tell you that it's a skill they've learned because they had to. Nina Hathway asks five people how they did it.

A   Jenny

When I left school I was very shy and I always thought I'd stay that way. I was about twenty-five when I was asked to help out at my daughter's school. I was sure I wouldn't cope, but I surprised myself by doing well and someone there suggested that I should do a university course.

There was a huge knot in my stomach the day I turned up for my first lecture. But my confidence gradually grew – I became more outgoing. Looking back, working at the school was the turning point in my life that has helped everything else fall into place.

B   Michaela

It all started four years ago when my father became ill and I had to take over the family business. I was so scared, I went over the top and became a bit too aggressive and impatient. I thought that was what confident people were like, but gradually I learned otherwise. To be confident you've got to believe in yourself.

If things get too demanding for me at work, I don't let myself feel guilty if I save a number of tasks until the next day. When I'm confronted with something difficult, I tell myself that I've got nothing to lose. It's fear that makes you lack confidence, so I'm always having quiet chats with myself to put aside those fears!

C   Carol

People think I'm very confident but, in fact, the calmer I look, the more terrified I really am. I've had to develop the ability to look confident because it's the most vital thing in TV. Interviewing people has helped me realise that most – if not all – of us get tense in important situations, and we feel calmer when we speak to someone who's genuinely friendly. The best ever piece of advice came from my mother when I was agonising as a teenager about wearing the right clothes. She simply cried, 'Who's looking at you? Everybody's too busy worrying

about how they look.' I've found that's well worth remembering.

I also think you gain confidence by tackling things that scare you. When I took my driving test I was so nervous, but I passed. After that I felt sure that I'd never feel so frightened again, and I never have.

D   Barbara

My confidence comes naturally from really enjoying the work I do, but it's something that I've built up over the years. If you just get on with it and learn from any mistakes you make, you're more confident the next time round. I work hard and I'm popular in the restaurant, but it's probable that one out of ten people doesn't like me. I don't let that affect me. You've got to like yourself for what you are, not try to be what others expect.

My company runs a lot of training courses, and going on those has built up my self-esteem. The company also encourages employees to set manageable targets. It helps no end if you can see you're achieving something tangible, rather than reaching for the stars all at once, and ending up with nothing but air!

E   Elaine

After I left college I worked for years as a secretary and would sit in meetings, not always agreeing with what was being said, but too scared to speak up. Eventually, I summoned up the confidence to start making my point. Even so, when I first worked in politics, I'd never spoken in public before and always used to shake like a leaf. I would say to myself, 'Don't be so silly. People do this every day of their lives, so there's no reason why you can't.' I also found it helpful to jot a few things down to refer to – rather like having a comfort blanket!

I don't think there is anyone who isn't a little shaky when it comes to talking publicly. The real secret of confidence lies in telling yourself over and over again, 'Nothing is impossible.'

PAPER 2   WRITING (1 hour 30 minutes)

Part 1

You **must** answer this question.

1   Your English friend, Peter, has written to you asking you to help him organise a special surprise birthday party for his sister, Anna.

Read Peter's letter and the notes you have made. Then, using all the information, write to Peter answering his questions **and** explaining how you think the party could be made special.

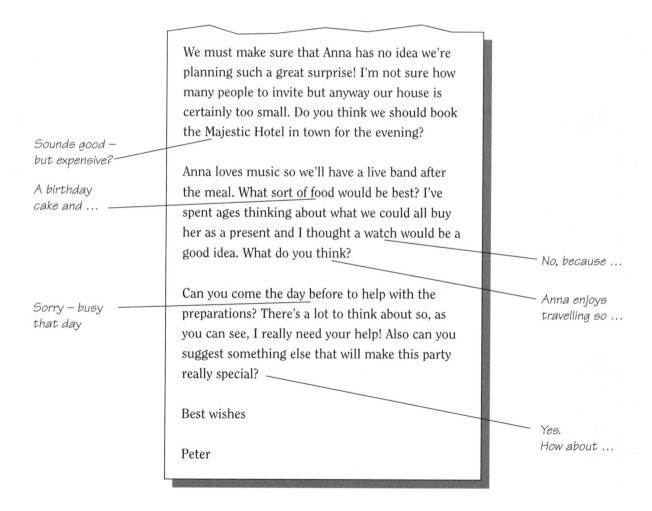

Sounds good – but expensive?

A birthday cake and …

Sorry – busy that day

We must make sure that Anna has no idea we're planning such a great surprise! I'm not sure how many people to invite but anyway our house is certainly too small. Do you think we should book the Majestic Hotel in town for the evening?

Anna loves music so we'll have a live band after the meal. What sort of food would be best? I've spent ages thinking about what we could all buy her as a present and I thought a watch would be a good idea. What do you think?

Can you come the day before to help with the preparations? There's a lot to think about so, as you can see, I really need your help! Also can you suggest something else that will make this party really special?

Best wishes

Peter

No, because …

Anna enjoys travelling so …

Yes. How about …

Write a **letter** of between **120** and **180** words in an appropriate style on the opposite page. Do not write any postal addresses.

Question 1

....
....
....
....
....
....
....
....
....
....
....
....
....
....
....
....
....
....
....
....
....
....
....
....
....
....
....
....
....
....

Part 2

Write an answer to **one** of the questions **2-5** in this part. Write your answer in **120-180** words in an appropriate style on the opposite page. Put the question number in the box.

2   You have been doing a class project on transport. Your teacher has now asked you to write a composition about the following statement:

There is no future for public transport, because travelling by car is so much more convenient.

Write your **composition**.

3   You see this advertisement for a job in the USA.

USA SUMMER CAMPS

People of all ages needed to work in summer camps all over the USA.

If you can speak English and you are cheerful, energetic and hardworking, you are the right person for us. Food and accommodation are provided. You just pay the air fare.

You will: – look after children aged 8–12
                        – help organise sports and evening activities
                        – work in the kitchens

Write telling us about yourself and why you think you would be a suitable person for the job.

Write your **letter of application**. Do not write any postal addresses.

4   An international student magazine is running a short story competition which you have decided to enter. The story must **end** with the following words:

Michael closed the door and knew at that moment he had made a mistake.

Write your **story**.

5   Answer **one** of the following two questions based on your reading of **one** of these set books. Write (**a**) or (**b**) as well as the number **5** in the question box, and the **title** of the book next to the box. Your answer **must** be about one of the books below.

Best Detective Stories of Agatha Christie – Longman Fiction
A Tale of Two Cities – Charles Dickens
Animal Farm – George Orwell
Wuthering Heights – Emily Brontë
More Tales from Shakespeare – Charles and Mary Lamb

Either (**a**) 'How important is the title of a book or short story?' Your teacher has asked you to write a **composition** discussing this question and explaining why the writer of the book or one of the short stories you have read chose that particular title.

Or   (**b**) The English book club you belong to is producing a list of books in English which it can recommend to members. The Club Secretary has asked you to write a **report** on the book or short stories you have read, saying whether this book would be suitable to include on the list and explaining why.

Question	

....
....
....
....
....
....
....
....
....
....
....
....
....
....
....
....
....
....
....
....
....
....
....
....
....
....
....
....
....
....

PAPER 3   USE OF ENGLISH (1 hour 15 minutes)

Part 1

For questions **1-15**, read the text below and decide which answer (**A**, **B**, **C** or **D**) best fits each space. There is an example at the beginning (**0**).

Mark your answers **on the separate answer sheet**.

Example:

0   **A**   celebrates   **B**   shows   **C**   honours   **D**   demonstrates

0	A	B	C	D

EVERYONE'S AN ARTIST

Every year, the village of Pettineo **(0)** ..... its unique arts festival. For a few days each summer, artists from all over Europe **(1)** ..... at this village near the north coast of Sicily to **(2)** ..... the creative atmosphere. During their stay, the artists get **(3)** ..... with the local people to paint a one-kilometre long picture that runs the **(4)** ..... of the high street. **(5)** ..... the painting is done, each visiting artist joins a local family for a big lunch and, **(6)** ..... the meal, the family receives the **(7)** ..... of the painting that the artist has painted. As a result, **(8)** ..... few villagers are rich, almost every home has at least one painting by a well-known European artist. Visitors to the village are eagerly **(9)** ..... into homes to see these paintings.

The festival was the **(10)** ..... of Antonio Presti, a local businessman who **(11)** ..... it up four years ago. Since then, Pettineo has **(12)** ..... a sort of domestic art museum in **(13)** ..... any visitor can ring a doorbell, go into a house and **(14)** ..... a painting. In addition to this exhibition of paintings in people's homes, for those who have time to spare, there is an opportunity to **(15)** ..... through the display of huge sculptures in the village square.

1 **A** group   **B** crowd   **C** gather   **D** combine

2 **A** amuse   **B** enjoy   **C** entertain   **D** delight

3 **A** linked   **B** jointly   **C** combined   **D** together

4 **A** size   **B** measure   **C** length   **D** area

5 **A** Just   **B** Once   **C** Soon   **D** Only

6 **A** in addition to   **B** in place of   **C** in common with **D** in exchange for

7 **A** partition   **B** section   **C** division   **D** region

8 **A** though   **B** despite   **C** since   **D** even

9 **A** persuaded   **B** invited   **C** requested   **D** attracted

10 **A** image   **B** purpose   **C** thought   **D** idea

11 **A** set   **B** put   **C** got   **D** had

12 **A** become   **B** advanced   **C** grown   **D** increased

13 **A** what   **B** where   **C** whom   **D** which

14 **A** wonder   **B** stare   **C** admire   **D** delight

15 **A** move   **B** step   **C** wander   **D** march

Part 2

For questions **16-30**, read the text below and think of the word which best fits each space. Use only **one** word in each space. There is an example at the beginning (**0**). Write your answers **on the separate answer sheet**.

Example: | **0** | *with* |

PROBLEMS FOR ACTORS

Many actors do not like working (**0**) ...*with*... children or animals. This is probably (**16**) .... they are afraid that the audience may become (**17**) .... interested in the children and animals than in them.

Actors can have problems (**18**) .... a different kind when they (**19**) .... required to eat or drink on stage. If they have (**20**) .... much food in their mouths, the words they say may not (**21**) .... clear, and they may even end up coughing and choking.

Other problems can occur with food (**22**) .... films are being made. In a recent film, during (**23**) .... a family was waiting to have a meal, one of the actors entered with a large roast chicken on a tray and then (**24**) .... to begin to cut some meat from it while he was speaking. By mistake, the actor cut off a whole leg of the chicken and then completely forgot (**25**) .... his next words were. It was necessary to film the scene (**26**) .... This (**27**) .... not really have mattered (**28**) .... there had been another roast chicken in the studio, but there was not. At (**29**) ...., nobody knew what to do, but eventually the problem was solved (**30**) .... putting a nail in the leg and attaching it back onto the chicken.

Part 3

For questions **31-40**, complete the second sentence so that it has a similar meaning to the first sentence, using the word given. **Do not change the word given**. You must use between **two** and **five** words, including the word given.

Here is an example (**0**).

Example:

0   You must do exactly what the manager tells you.

carry

You must .... instructions exactly.

The gap can be filled by the words 'carry out the manager's' so you write:

| 0 | *carry out the manager's* |

Write **only the missing words** on the separate answer sheet.

---

31   John is interested in knowing more about astronomy.

like

John .... more about astronomy.

32   Because of the parade, we weren't allowed to park in the High Street.

let

Because of the parade, the police wouldn't .... in the High Street.

33   'Did you see that film on television on Saturday?' Susan asked me.

seen

Susan wanted to know .... that film on television on Saturday.

34   'I'm afraid these jeans have a hole in them.'

there

'I'm afraid that .... these jeans.'

35 They cancelled the match because of the bad weather.

called

The match .... because of the bad weather.

36 Dan never takes any notice of my advice.

attention

Dan never .... my advice.

37 'Can I borrow your bicycle, Sarah?' asked Frank.

lend

Frank asked Sarah .... her bicycle.

38 Maybe Peter forgot that we changed the time of the meeting.

might

Peter .... that we changed the time of the meeting.

39 She checks the company accounts very efficiently.

efficient

She's very .... the company accounts.

40 All the children enjoy themselves at this summer camp.

fun

Every .... at this summer camp.

Part 4

For questions **41-55**, read the text below and look carefully at each line. Some of the lines are correct, and some have a word which should not be there.

If a line is correct, put a tick (✓) by the number **on the separate answer sheet**. If a line has a word which should **not** be there, write the word **on the separate answer sheet**. There are two examples at the beginning (**0** and **00**).

Examples:

0	✓
00	*of*

A LETTER OF COMPLAINT

0	I am writing to complain about our recent holiday, which involved
00	several last-minute changes to the arrangements, despite of the fact
41	that we had made our booking for several months in advance.
42	The journey to the coast took four hours longer than your
43	brochure suggested. The coach which took us was far too much old
44	and the last part of the journey was terrifying, as if the driver tried to
45	make up for the time we had lost. However, this was nothing
46	compared with our own horror when we arrived at the hotel. Your
47	advertisement promised to us large rooms with colour television. In fact,
48	our bedroom was hardly that big enough to lie down in and the only
49	television was in the lounge. We did not go downstairs for eat an evening
50	meal, but decided instead to go to the bed straightaway.
51	It was quite clear that we could not enjoy our holiday in this hotel.
52	Your representative was no help at all, so we had to find
53	somewhere else to stay at for the rest of the week ourselves.
54	I expect you to return the money we paid for this trip, which it totally
55	failed to live up to the claims made in your brochure.

Part 5

For questions **56-65**, read the text below. Use the word given in capitals at the end of each line to form a word that fits in the space in the same line. There is an example at the beginning (**0**). Write your answers **on the separate answer sheet**.

Example: | **0** | *growth* |

AIRPORTS

With the (**0**) .*growth*. in air travel, airports have become symbols of   **GROW**

international importance, and are (**56**) ..... designed by well-known   **FREQUENT**

architects. Airports have (**57**) ..... facilities nowadays.   **IMPRESS**

There are (**58**) ..... departure lounges, where passengers wait   **COMFORT**

before boarding their (**59**) ..... , restaurants, shopping areas and   **FLY**

banks. Good road and rail (**60**) ..... with nearby towns and cities are also   **COMMUNICATE**

essential.

However, it is becoming (**61**) ..... difficult to find land on   **INCREASE**

which to build airports, as aircraft, despite (**62**) ..... in   **IMPROVE**

engine design, are (**63**) ..... , and need a considerable amount of   **NOISE**

space in which to land and take off. (**64**) ..... residential areas   **CROWD**

need to be avoided, so, (**65**) ..... , suitable land might be an   **FORTUNATE**

inconvenient distance away from the city.

PAPER 4   LISTENING (approximately 40 minutes)

Part 1

You will hear people talking in eight different situations. For questions **1-8**, choose the best answer (**A**, **B** or **C**).

1   You overhear two people talking in a restaurant.
Where has the woman just come from?

   A   a supermarket

   B   a hospital

   C   a football match

	1

2   You hear a man talking about a mobile phone he has bought.
What most attracted him to this phone?

   A   its size

   B   its reliability

   C   its price

	2

3   You hear a man talking on the phone about buying a house.
What is the purpose of his call?

   A   to apologise

   B   to complain

   C   to obtain information

	3

4   You hear a teenage girl talking about her hobby.
What is she talking about?

   A   a computer game

   B   a musical instrument

   C   a piece of sports equipment

	4

5 On the news, you hear a story about a cat.
Where was the cat found?

    A in a train carriage

    B on the railway lines

    C on a station platform

        5

6 You hear a woman talking about how she gets ideas for her work.
Who is the woman?

    A a novelist

    B an artist

    C a film-maker

        6

7 You hear two people talking.
How does the woman feel?

    A surprised

    B satisfied

    C relieved

        7

8 You turn on the radio and hear a man speaking.
What are you listening to?

    A a history programme

    B a science-fiction story

    C an advertisement

        8

Part 2

You will hear a radio interview with a woman who is organising a training weekend for people interested in the theatre. For questions **9-18**, complete the notes.

TRAINING WEEKEND

WHEN: beginning of [_____ **9**]

CONTENT: Saturday – two groups run by professionals

                 subjects: [_____ **10**] or directing

                 Sunday – two groups

                 subjects: make-up or press and [_____ **11**]

WHERE: mostly [_____ **12**] (at the theatre)

COST: whole weekend course (if booked):

                 [_____ **13**] (includes lunches)

COURSE LEADERS: have training as [_____ **14**]

MAIN AGE GROUP: [_____ **15**]

LAST YEAR'S TRAINING DAY: concentrated on [_____ **16**]

HOW TO APPLY: name of person to phone: Claire [_____ **17**]

                     official position of person:

                     [_____ **18**] (at the theatre)

Part 3

You will hear five different students who are studying away from home. They are talking about their accommodation. For questions **19-23**, choose from the list (**A-F**) what each speaker says about their accommodation. Use the letters only once. There is one extra letter which you do not need to use.

A   I made a mistake there at first.

Speaker 1	19

B   I was able to settle into a new area.

Speaker 2	20

C   I had no choice in the matter.

Speaker 3	21

D   I have recommended it to others.

Speaker 4	22

E   There are more benefits than disadvantages.

Speaker 5	23

F   I would prefer to have more freedom.

Part 4

You will hear part of a radio interview in which Tina White, a magazine editor, talks about her life and work. For questions **24-30**, choose the best answer (**A**, **B** or **C**).

---

24   In her first column, Tina chose to write about people who

    A   were very well known.

    B   had interesting ideas.

    C   lived in luxury.

                        24

25   She took up journalism because of

    A   her family connections.

    B   her father's support.

    C   her love for books.

                        25

26   Under her management, the magazine *Female Focus*

    A   reduced its losses.

    B   changed its image.

    C   made a profit.

                        26

27   She believes people are more likely to read an article if

    A   it has a good beginning.

    B   its content is challenging.

    C   it is mentioned on the cover.

                        27

28   When she started her present job five years ago, she

    A   organised her ideal team.

    B   had more time to read everything.

    C   lacked confidence in her staff.

                        28

29   Tina says that she would be worried if she

    A   was criticised by the public.

    B   lost the respect of colleagues.

    C   lost her job.

                        29

30   In the future, she would like to

    A   be a book editor.

    B   produce a film.

    C   write fiction.

                        30

PAPER 5 SPEAKING (14 minutes)

You take the Speaking test with another candidate, referred to here as your partner. There are two examiners. One will speak to you and your partner and the other will be listening. Both examiners will award marks.

Part 1 (3 minutes)

The examiner asks you and your partner questions about yourselves. You may be asked about things like 'your home town', 'your interests', 'your career plans', etc.

Part 2 (4 minutes)

The examiner gives you two photographs and asks you to talk about them for one minute. The examiner then asks your partner a question about your photographs and your partner responds briefly.

Then the examiner gives your partner two different photographs. Your partner talks about these photographs for one minute. This time the examiner asks you a question about your partner's photographs and you respond briefly.

Part 3 (approximately 3 minutes)

The examiner asks you and your partner to talk together. You may be asked to solve a problem or try to come to a decision about something. For example, you might be asked to decide the best way to use some rooms in a language school. The examiner gives you a picture to help you but does not join in the conversation.

Part 4 (approximately 4 minutes)

The examiner joins in the conversation. You all talk together in a more general way about what has been said in Part 3. The examiner asks you questions but you and your partner are also expected to develop the conversation.

Test 3

PAPER 1   READING (1 hour 15 minutes)

Part 1

You are going to read a magazine article about human behaviour. Choose from the list **A-I** the sentence which best summarises each part (**1-7**) of the article. There is one extra sentence which you do not need to use. There is an example at the beginning (**0**).

Mark your answers **on the separate answer sheet**.

A   People are very keen to be skilful at misleading others.

B   People are sometimes unable to hide the fact that they are being dishonest.

C   Instinct plays an important part in our development.

D   People seldom realise that their faces are showing that they are being dishonest.

E   It is not easy for anyone to detect dishonesty.

F   People form judgements about other people just by looking at their faces.

G   Being good at fooling others may be a sign of high intelligence.

H   The way that feelings are shown is common to a great many people.

I   It is strange that people often do not realise when others are being dishonest with them.

Facing the truth

*Our facial expressions provide a clear map of our emotions.
But some people cannot read the signposts ...*

0 | **I**

Our brains have been processing sophisticated information via our senses for millions of years. So why is it we are still vulnerable to lies? Why aren't we better at discovering the deception of others?

1

The language of the face is emotion. Almost our first sight as a new-born baby is our mother's face smiling at us. Not only are we immediately programmed to respond to faces, but right away we can also signal surprise, pleasure and distress. The constant visual dialogue, as parent and child mirror expressions back and forth, is vital for the young brain. It is how we build a sense of other minds – we feel happy when we smile, so someone else smiling must be feeling the same.

2

Not only is the emotional language of the face vital to normal functioning, it also seems to be almost universal, says Paul Ekman, a leading researcher in the subject. 'Wherever you are, anger, happiness, fear, disgust, sadness and surprise look the same.'

3

But we make all sorts of false assumptions about faces. Attractive people, for instance, may get the benefit of the doubt. We sometimes assume they are kinder, cleverer and more honest than those with less regular features. Then we have other unconscious biases about certain kinds of face. In a woman, certain facial features may be thought attractive, but the same features may mark a man out as weak.

4

These are just some of the ways we fool ourselves. So why aren't we better at detecting liars? Because for millions of years humans have been in a battle with each other to develop better techniques for deception. We are highly social animals and our survival depends not only on cooperating with others but also on getting an advantage when we can. In fact, one theory claims that the ability to cheat, to make others in the group think an expression means friendship rather than anger, is one of the most important factors driving human development.

5

Some believe it is also related to how bright we are. 'We have found a strong relationship between the ability to deceive and brain power,' says Leda Cosmides, a psychologist at the University of California. 'The more developed people's minds are, the better they are at concealing their intentions and manipulating others for their own ends.'

6

Humans are simply the biggest liars on the planet and we start lying convincingly from a very early age. Studies show that even people who deal with deception professionally, such as judges and policemen, score only about 50% – the same as the rest of us – when asked to rate people as to whether they are telling the truth or not on videotape.

7

Our voices, however, can betray our intention. Dr Richard Williams of Hereford University has found that when people are blindfolded, they can spot the difference between someone telling the truth and a lie about 75% of the time. 'Most people, when they are lying, are rarely aware that they've started to speak more softly or more slowly,' he says.

Part 2

You are going to read an article about a man who makes works of art out of sea shells. For questions **8-15**, choose the answer (**A**, **B**, **C** or **D**) which you think fits best according to the text.

Mark your answers **on the separate answer sheet**.

THE SHELL ARTIST

At the age of 83 Peter Cooke has become a master of his art.

There are still many things that Peter Cooke would like to try his hand at – paper-making and feather-work are on his list. For the moment though, he will stick to the skill that he has been delighted to perfect over the past ten years: making delicate and unusual objects out of shells.

'Tell me if I am boring you,' he says, as he leads me round his apartment showing me his work. There is a fine line between being a bore and being an enthusiast, but Cooke need not worry: he fits into the latter category, helped both by his charm and by the beauty of the things he makes.

He points to a pair of shell-covered ornaments above a fireplace. 'I shan't be at all bothered if people don't buy them because I have got so used to them, and to me they're adorable. I never meant to sell my work commercially. Some friends came to see me about five years ago and said, "You must have an exhibition – people ought to see these. We'll talk to a man who owns an art gallery".' The result was an exhibition in London, at which 70 per cent of the objects were sold. His second exhibition opened at the gallery yesterday. Considering the enormous prices the pieces command – around £2,000 for the ornaments – an empty space above the
25 fireplace would seem a small sacrifice for Cooke to make.

There are 86 pieces in the exhibition, with prices starting at £225 for a shell-flower in a crystal vase. Cooke insists that he has nothing to do with the prices and is cheerily open about their level: he claims there is nobody else in the world who produces work like his, and, as the gallery-owner told him, 'Well, you're going to stop one day and everybody will want your pieces because there won't be any more.'

'I do wish, though,' says Cooke, 'that I'd taken this up a lot earlier, because then I would have been able to

produce really wonderful things – at least the potential would have been there. Although the ideas are still there and I'm doing the best I can now, I'm more limited physically than I was when I started.' Still, the work that he has managed to produce is a long way from the common shell constructions that can be found in seaside shops. 'I have a miniature mind,' he says, and this has resulted in boxes covered in thousands of tiny shells, little shaded pictures made from shells and baskets of astonishingly realistic flowers.

Cooke has created his own method and uses materials as and when he finds them. He uses the cardboard sent back with laundered shirts for his flower bases, a nameless glue bought in bulk from a sail-maker ('If it runs out, I don't know what I will do!') and washing-up liquid to wash the shells. 'I have an idea of what I want to do, and it just does itself,' he says of his working method, yet the attention to detail, colour gradations and symmetry he achieves look far from accidental.

Cooke's quest for beautiful, and especially tiny, shells has taken him further than his Norfolk shore: to France, Thailand, Mexico, South Africa and the Philippines, to name but a few of the beaches where he has lain on his stomach and looked for beauties to bring home. He is insistent that he only collects dead shells and defends himself against people who write him letters accusing him of stripping the world's beaches. 'When I am collecting shells, I hear people's great fat feet crunching them up far faster than I can collect them; and the ones that are left, the sea breaks up. I would not dream of collecting shells with living creatures in them or diving for them, but once their occupants have left, why should I not collect them?' If one bases this argument on the amount of luggage that can be carried home by one man, the sum beauty of whose work is often greater than its natural parts, it becomes very convincing indeed. 72

8   What does the reader learn about Peter Cooke in the first paragraph?

   A   He has produced hand-made objects in different materials.

   B   He was praised for his shell objects many years ago.

   C   He hopes to work with other materials in the future.

   D   He has written about his love of making shell objects.

9   When looking round his apartment, the writer

   A   is attracted by Cooke's personality.

   B   senses that Cooke wants his products to be admired.

   C   realises he finds Cooke's work boring.

   D   feels uncertain about giving Cooke his opinion.

10   The 'small sacrifice' in line 25 refers to

   A   the loss of Cooke's ornaments.

   B   the display of Cooke's ornaments.

   C   the cost of keeping Cooke's ornaments.

   D   the space required to store Cooke's ornaments.

11   When the writer enquires about the cost of his shell objects, Cooke

   A   cleverly changes the subject.

   B   defends the prices charged for his work.

   C   says he has no idea why the level is so high.

   D   notes that his work will not always be so popular.

12   What does Cooke regret about his work?

   A   He is not as famous as he should have been.

   B   He makes less money than he should make.

   C   He is less imaginative than he used to be.

   D   He is not as skilful as he used to be.

13   When talking about the artist's working method, the writer suspects that Cooke

   A   accepts that he sometimes makes mistakes.

   B   is unaware of the unique quality his work has.

   C   underrates his creative contribution.

   D   undervalues the materials that he uses.

14   What does the reader learn about Cooke's shell-collecting activities?

   A   Not everyone approves of what he does.

   B   Other methods might make his work easier.

   C   Other tourists get in the way of his collecting.

   D   Not all shells are the right size and shape for his work.

15   What does 'it' in line 72 refer to?

   A   Cooke's luggage

   B   Cooke's argument

   C   the beauty of Cooke's work

   D   the reason for Cooke's trips

Part 3

You are going to read a magazine article about a new hotel. Eight sentences have been removed from the article. Choose from the sentences **A-I** the one which fits each gap (**16-22**). There is one extra sentence which you do not need to use. There is an example at the beginning (**0**).

Mark your answers **on the separate answer sheet**.

Five-star luxury meets up-to-date technology

The five-star Merrion Hotel, which has just opened, is the result of considerable research into customer requirements and nearly two years' work converting four large, eighteenth-century houses in Dublin. **0** | **I** | This has been done for the benefit of staff and guests alike.

At the Merrion, General Manager Peter MacCann expects his staff to know the guests by name. **16** | | It can deal with return clients in the extra-special way that is appropriate to a five-star hotel.

Though the system cost £250,000 to install, it will pay for itself over time, according to MacCann. **17** | | For example, a guest who requests certain music CDs during a first stay will find those same CDs ready for him on a return visit. This is thanks to the guest-history facility which allows staff to key in any number of preferences.

Hotel guests the world over frequently complain about room temperature. **18** | | Guests have the opportunity to change the temperature themselves within three degrees either side of the normal 18°C but, in addition, each individual room can be adjusted by any amount between 14°C and 25°C at the front desk.

19 | | This is particularly true for the business user, and MacCann estimates that up to sixty-five per cent of his business will come from this part of the market. To provide the best service for such needs, the hotel has taken the traditional business centre and put it into individual bedrooms. Each one has three phones, two phone lines, a fax machine that doubles as a photocopier and printer, and a video-conferencing facility.

Technology changes so quickly these days that the hotel has had to try to forecast possible improvements. **20** | | The televisions are rented rather than bought, so that they can be replaced with more up-to-date models at any time. Video recorders can also be upgraded when necessary.

Despite the presence of all this very up-to-the-minute equipment in the rooms, MacCann says they have tried hard not to make guests feel threatened by the technology. | **21** | There are, of course, a swimming pool and gym, six conference rooms, two bars and two restaurants, and a beautiful garden at the heart of it all.

As at all luxury hotels, the food that is offered to guests must be excellent. Chef Patrick Guilbaud's Dublin restaurant already had two Michelin stars when he agreed to move his restaurant business to the Merrion. | **22** | He has been able to design a new kitchen and take it into the modern age. There are better parking facilities than at the previous address, too. From the hotel's side, they are able to offer a popular and successful place to eat, with no financial risks attached.

Aided by technology and a highly capable staff, the Merrion looks likely to succeed.

A For guests, though, it is the other technology offered in their rooms which is most likely to find favour.

B Being part of the hotel site has huge benefits, both for him and the hotel itself.

C Extra cables have been laid to handle whatever scientific advances may occur.

D He expects fifty per cent of the rooms to be occupied in the hotel's first year.

E Another hi-tech system controls this essential area of comfort.

F However, for details of his guests' preferences, he relies on the hotel's computer system.

G The one hundred and forty-five bedrooms, large and well-furnished, are both comfortable and welcoming.

H He praises its efficiency and talks enthusiastically of the facilities it offers.

I Creating a new hotel in this way has allowed the latest technology to be installed.

Part 4

You are going to read a magazine article about members of a part-time drama club called The Globe Players. For questions **23-35**, choose from the people (**A-F**). The people may be chosen more than once. When more than one answer is required, these may be given in any order. There is an example at the beginning (**0**).

Mark your answers **on the separate answer sheet**.

Which person or people

mentions joining because of loneliness?	**0** A	
had some theatre experience before joining The Globe Players?	**23**	
has a high opinion of The Globe Players?	**24**	
believes the other members are like them in character?	**25**	
has mixed feelings about finishing a show?	**26**	
have difficulty finding suitable roles?	**27**	**28**
enjoys being with people who have different ideas?	**29**	
thinks that acting is out of character for them?	**30**	
mentions the publicity they sometimes receive?	**31**	
joined to keep busy?	**32**	
talks about the complications of putting on a play?	**33**	
feel that not everyone approves of them acting?	**34**	**35**

The Globe Players

A Christina Howard

When I moved to this area the children were quite little, and I wondered how I was ever going to meet people. Then I met Susanna Dickster, who was the organiser of The Globe Players, and she said, 'Do you want to join?' And I said, 'Well, yes, all right.' They appeared to be incredibly extrovert people, which I suppose I am by nature too. For three years I was the theatre manager. I think I make a better manager than an actress, but I did have a dream role in a play the year before last.

B Eric Plumber

I do about one play a year, just out of interest. But I'm a quiet sort of chap, not one of the world's extroverts, and yet here I am in an extrovert field, doing theatrical activities. There is a sort of magic to the theatre. There's a sense of togetherness with the rest of the actors in the cast. When a play is over, on the last night, there's a combination of anticlimax and relief. It's rather nice to think you will be able to do all the things that you weren't able to do when the play was on. But there's also a sense of loss, so you look forward to the next play.

C Laura Goldcrest

I have done some stage management for productions at my school and when I saw the play The Globe Players were going to do next, I thought I'd try for it. Usually there are not a lot of parts for people my age, so when there was this opportunity, I went along and auditioned. It went all right, and I got the part. Lots of my friends just hang around with people of their own age, but there are people at The Globe Players who are quite old, and I get talking to them about all sorts of things. It's amazing how our views differ, but we have lovely conversations.

D Clare MacDonald

When I was at school, I used to think I'd rather like to go on stage. But then other things came along. One job I did was as a stewardess for an airline. That's like giving a performance. I left the airline and joined The Globe Players. My husband will always come to performances, but he does tend to moan a bit because he feels it takes up too much time. As a club I feel we are very professional. I do about one play a year, which is quite enough. Obviously, there are fewer parts as you get older, particularly for women: one can no longer play Juliet or other young parts, which I feel sad about.

E Robin Wilson

I work behind the scenes with The Globe Players because it's always a challenge. For instance, the last play I did needed a full-sized, working swimming pool. Well, most amateur theatres have a bucket of water in the wings. But our director said, 'I want a real swimming pool on that set. Go away and do it.' It was a real challenge for me. However, we did it. We got more reviews than we usually do because, of course, it was something different. And quite a lot of amateur societies came to see if they could do it – and a lot of them decided they couldn't.

F Mike James

I was a science teacher and took early retirement from my college. After twenty-four years it was a bit hard and I got rather bored. During that time it was good to have the drama group. It takes your mind off things; you can't act and worry about something else. But it's very disruptive to a family – my wife will tell you that. Teaching in a way is like being on stage. When you go into a class you may not be feeling very well, you are not necessarily very keen on the subject you are teaching – the whole thing adds up to a no-no. But you go in, you are enthusiastic and you try to generate interest, and it's an act.

PAPER 2   WRITING (1 hour 30 minutes)

Part 1

You **must** answer this question.

1   You are studying in Britain and you have recently received a letter from an English friend who is interested in arranging a day trip for a group of students.

Read the extract from your friend's letter and the advertisement for a boat trip, on which you have made some notes. Then, using all your notes, write a letter to your friend giving the information requested and saying whether you would recommend the trip.

> *The students in my class are really interested in going on a day trip. I know you went on a boat trip with your English class recently. Could you tell me what it was like and whether you'd recommend it?*

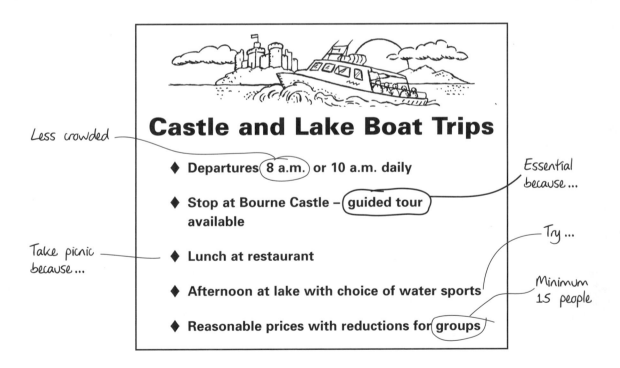

Write a **letter** of between **120** and **180** words in an appropriate style on the opposite page. Do not write any postal addresses.

Question 1

Part 2

Write an answer to **one** of the questions **2-5** in this part. Write your answer in **120-180** words in an appropriate style on the opposite page. Put the question number in the box.

2   An English language club is starting in your area. The organisers of the club have asked you to write a report giving your suggestions about:

• how often the club should meet
• what type of activities it should organise
• how the club could be advertised

Write your **report**.

3   You have decided to enter a short story competition in an international magazine. The competition rules say that the story must **begin** with the following words:

It was three o'clock in the morning when the phone rang.

Write your **story**.

4   You have seen this announcement in *Leisure and Entertainment* magazine.

Could you live without television for a week?

Write and tell us what difference this would make to your life.

We will publish the best article.

Write your **article**.

5   Answer **one** of the following two questions based on your reading of **one** of these set books. Write (**a**) or (**b**) as well as the number **5** in the question box, and the **title** of the book next to the box. Your answer **must** be about one of the books below.

Best Detective Stories of Agatha Christie – Longman Fiction
A Tale of Two Cities – Charles Dickens
Animal Farm – George Orwell
Wuthering Heights – Emily Brontë
More Tales from Shakespeare – Charles and Mary Lamb

Either (**a**)   'Did anything in the book or short story you have read disappoint you?' Write a **composition**, answering this question with reference to the book or one of the short stories you have read.

Or (**b**)   'For a book to be successful, the author has to show the importance of the relationships between characters.' Is this true of the book or one of the short stories you have read? Write a **composition**, explaining your views.

Question

....
....
....
....
....
....
....
....
....
....
....
....
....
....
....
....
....
....
....
....
....
....
....
....
....
....
....
....
....
....
....

PAPER 3   USE OF ENGLISH (1 hour 15 minutes)

Part 1

For questions **1-15**, read the text below and decide which answer (**A**, **B**, **C** or **D**) best fits each space. There is an example at the beginning (**0**).

Mark your answers **on the separate answer sheet**.

Example:

0   A   speed   **B**   pace   **C**   rate   **D**   rhythm

0	A	B	C	D
	—	—	—	—

THE NEED FOR BIGGER PLANES

The big issue for plane-makers planning for the future is size, not **(0)** ..... . With the skies already full of air traffic, and with worse to **(1)** ..... , the important questions for the designers are how many passengers they can **(2)** ..... into the new super-planes and who will be **(3)** ..... to build them first.

(4) ..... yourself ten years from now in a packed airport departure lounge. Eight hundred passengers are waiting with you for their first flight on one of a remarkable range of super-planes, and the check-in time **(5)** ..... have been as much as four hours before take-off to **(6)** ..... for the extra people. Impossible? Far from it. Designs for these planes are already **(7)** ..... on computer at the world's top aircraft manufacturers, waiting to be turned **(8)** ..... reality.

The airlines badly need the new jets to **(9)** ..... with future increases in passenger **(10)** ..... . A billion passengers a year are currently carried by air, but that figure is **(11)** ..... to double by the year 2010. The only practical **(12)** ..... of avoiding making the skies even busier is to build much bigger planes. The **(13)** ..... to build the new jets is the hottest contest in the airliner business. Manufacturers are working **(14)** ..... with the major airlines to produce designs that will please airlines and passengers **(15)** ..... .

1 **A** go   **B** happen   **C** come   **D** arrive

2 **A** contain   **B** fit   **C** hold   **D** sit

3 **A** possible   **B** able   **C** proper   **D** capable

4 **A** Consider   **B** Suppose   **C** Imagine   **D** Regard

5 **A** can   **B** need   **C** ought   **D** may

6 **A** watch   **B** allow   **C** look   **D** permit

7 **A** supplied   **B** given   **C** stored   **D** carried

8 **A** as   **B** by   **C** into   **D** for

9 **A** deal   **B** treat   **C** manage   **D** succeed

10 **A** amounts   **B** sums   **C** quantities **D** numbers

11 **A** expected   **B** thought   **C** known   **D** hoped

12 **A** scheme   **B** process   **C** way   **D** plan

13 **A** game   **B** sport   **C** match   **D** race

14 **A** tightly   **B** strongly   **C** closely   **D** firmly

15 **A** equal   **B** alike   **C** similar   **D** same

Part 2

For questions **16-30**, read the text below and think of the word which best fits each space. Use only **one** word in each space. There is an example at the beginning (**0**).
Write your answers **on the separate answer sheet**.

Example: | **0** | *his* |

CHARLES DICKENS' CHILDHOOD EXPERIENCES

Charles Dickens was one of the greatest nineteenth-century English novelists. At the time of (**0**) ...*his*.... death in 1870 he was a wealthy man, in contrast to the poverty of his early days. His parents (**16**) .... their best to look after him but were always in difficulties (**17**) .... money. Eventually, his father owed (**18**) .... a large amount of money that he was sent to prison for three months.

Two days after his twelfth birthday, Dickens was taken away from school by his parents and made (**19**) .... work in a factory in London to increase the family income. Factories could be dangerous places in (**20**) .... days and some employers were cruel. Charles was not (**21**) .... extremely unhappy, but also ashamed of working there, and he (**22**) .... never forget that period of his life. Years later, (**23**) .... his novel 'Oliver Twist', Dickens described his own childhood experiences. Oliver Twist was one of his most famous characters and he too suffered (**24**) .... a child worker. Dickens' novels showed how shocking working and living conditions (**25**) .... Working in the factory affected him so deeply that he found (**26**) .... much too painful to speak about in later life. His own wife and children knew (**27**) .... at all about the unhappiness of his childhood while Dickens was still alive, (**28**) .... shortly after his death a biography was published in (**29**) .... Dickens' terrible childhood experiences in the factory were revealed (**30**) .... the first time.

Part 3

For questions **31-40**, complete the second sentence so that it has a similar meaning to the first sentence, using the word given. **Do not change the word given**. You must use between **two** and **five** words, including the word given.

Here is an example (**0**).

Example:

0   You must do exactly what the manager tells you.

carry

You must .... instructions exactly.

The gap can be filled by the words 'carry out the manager's' so you write:

| **0** | *carry out the manager's* |

Write **only the missing words** on the separate answer sheet.

---

31   How many cars can this company produce in a month?

by

How many cars can .... in a month?

32   'That's the last time I talk to him!' Geoff said.

again

'I'm not going .... !' Geoff said.

33   While I was on holiday, a lot of interesting things happened to me.

my

During .... a lot of interesting experiences.

34   It was careless of you to leave without locking the door.

ought

You .... the door before you left.

35 'Is Pete likely to change his mind?' Rob asked.

chance

'Is there .... changing his mind?' Rob asked.

36 Paul is the only person who has replied to the invitation.

nobody

Apart .... replied to the invitation.

37 Are you familiar with his teaching style yet?

used

Have you .... his teaching style yet?

38 It was such a sunny day that none of us wanted to do any work.

felt

None of us .... any work because it was such a sunny day.

39 Barbara couldn't sing or dance.

unable

Besides .... , Barbara couldn't dance either.

40 Dinner will be served immediately upon our arrival at the hotel.

soon

Dinner will be served .... at the hotel.

Part 4

For questions **41-55**, read the text below and look carefully at each line. Some of the lines are correct, and some have a word which should not be there.

If a line is correct, put a tick (✓) by the number **on the separate answer sheet**. If a line has a word which should **not** be there, write the word **on the separate answer sheet**. There are two examples at the beginning (**0** and **00**).

Examples:

0	*am*
00	✔

REPORT ON AN ENGLISH LANGUAGE COURSE

0	In July of this year I am spent one month on an intensive English
00	language course in Melchester, in the north of England. The course
41	was held place in a modern building which was equipped with a
42	new language laboratory and a library. There were being also
43	good sports facilities. Lessons began at 9.00 in every morning and
44	have finished at 12.00. There was an hour's lunch break, after
45	which we had the choice of working in the library, by going on
46	a visit to somewhere of interest in Melchester or joining one
47	of the optional afternoon classes. The class I went to which was
48	the Business English course, and I would say that it had certainly
49	helped me to write either letters and reports in English. Every
50	weekend, excursions there were arranged to other parts of Britain,
51	including a long weekend in York, which it was very enjoyable
52	despite of the poor weather. The month was certainly useful
53	not only because my spoken English having improved, but also
54	because I learned too many things about English life and culture.
55	Everyone who uses English in his or her work would benefit from this course.

Part 5

For questions **56-65**, read the text below. Use the word given in capitals at the end of each line to form a word that fits in the space in the same line. There is an example at the beginning (**0**). Write your answers **on the separate answer sheet**.

Example: | **0** | *extremely* |

THE LONDON UNDERGROUND MAP

The London Underground map is **(0)** *extremely*. well designed.	**EXTREME**
Simple, easy to understand and **(56)** ..... , it performs its primary task of	**ATTRACT**
guiding both inhabitants and **(57)** ..... round the underground system in London	**TOUR**
very well. The man behind this great **(58)** ..... was called Henry Beck,	**ACHIEVE**
an **(59)** ..... of the London Underground Drawing Office, who designed the	**EMPLOY**
map in 1931. The design of the map showed great **(60)** ..... because it	**ORIGINAL**
represented a complex network of **(61)** ..... clearly. This design was	**COMMUNICATE**
later used by most of the world's underground systems.	

The map used before 1931 was messy and **(62)** ..... . So Beck decided to	**CLEAR**
sketch out a better one using a diagram rather than a **(63)** ..... map. This new	**TRADITION**
map was an enormous **(64)** ..... with the public when, in 1933, it made its first	**SUCCEED**
(65) ..... on underground platforms and at station entrances.	**APPEAR**

PAPER 4   LISTENING (approximately 40 minutes)

Part 1

You will hear people talking in eight different situations. For questions **1-8**, choose the best answer (**A**, **B** or **C**).

1   You overhear a man talking about an experience he had at an airport.
    What did he lose?

   A   his passport

   B   his wallet

   C   a piece of luggage

   > 1

2   You hear an advertisement on the radio.
    What is special about the *Fretlight* guitar?

   A   It plays recorded music.

   B   It teaches you how to play.

   C   It plugs into a computer.

   > 2

3   You hear part of a radio programme.
    What is the presenter talking about?

   A   food safety

   B   meal times

   C   healthy recipes

   > 3

4   You hear two people discussing a type of pollution.
    What do the speakers agree about?

   A   the best way to solve the problem

   B   how they feel about this type of pollution

   C   how they reacted to the solution they saw

   > 4

5 You hear a conversation between a shop assistant and a customer about a compact disc.
What was the cause of the problem?

A The customer gave the wrong number.

B A mistake was made on the order form.

C The disc was incorrectly labelled.

	5

6 You overhear a conversation at a football game.
What does the speaker say about his team?

A They're better than usual.

B They're as good as he expected.

C They tend to be unlucky.

	6

7 You overhear a schoolgirl talking to her friend.
What does she think about her new teacher?

A He is clever.

B He is funny.

C He is interesting.

	7

8 In a hotel you overhear a conversation.
Who is the woman?

A a tour guide

B a tourist

C a hotel receptionist

	8

Part 2

You will hear part of a radio interview with a swimming instructor. For questions **9-18**, complete the sentences.

Paul works at a hotel in the ☐ **9**

He started his job in ☐ **10**

He particularly likes meeting ☐ **11** there.

Paul isn't interested in teaching ☐ **12**

According to Paul, ☐ **13** of all adults can't swim.

Paul's students are afraid of going ☐ **14**

His students have to put their faces into a salad bowl and ☐ **15**

below the surface.

The first thing they do in the pool is to ☐ **16**

in the water with their faces down.

Paul thinks it's essential to be ☐ **17** in the water.

Most people learn to swim after about ☐ **18**

Part 3

You will hear part of a radio programme called *Morning Market*. Five listeners have telephoned the programme because they have something to sell. For questions **19-23**, choose which of the statements (**A-F**) matches the reason each of the people gives for selling their possession. Use the letters only once. There is one extra letter which you do not need to use.

A   I didn't enjoy using it.

Speaker 1   **19**

B   I made a mistake.

Speaker 2   **20**

C   It's an unwanted prize.

Speaker 3   **21**

D   It takes up too much space.

Speaker 4   **22**

E   I've got something better.

Speaker 5   **23**

F   I have health problems.

Part 4

You will hear a radio interview with Peter Manson about the job he does for a record company. For questions **24-30**, decide which of the statements are TRUE and which are FALSE. Write **T** for **TRUE** or **F** for **FALSE**.

---

24   In the 1980s, record companies could not find new musicians. | 24

25   Peter's job is difficult because most young artists are shy. | 25

26   Peter was unwilling at first to give a contract to the band he saw in a tent. | 26

27   Some bands send him expensive presents. | 27

28   He was forced to listen to a tape containing threats. | 28

29   He tends to spend only a short time at a show. | 29

30   He signed a contract with one band without hearing them sing. | 30

PAPER 5   SPEAKING (14 minutes)

You take the Speaking test with another candidate, referred to here as your partner. There are two examiners. One will speak to you and your partner and the other will be listening. Both examiners will award marks.

Part 1 (3 minutes)

The examiner asks you and your partner questions about yourselves. You may be asked about things like 'your home town', 'your interests', 'your career plans', etc.

Part 2 (4 minutes)

The examiner gives you two photographs and asks you to talk about them for one minute. The examiner then asks your partner a question about your photographs and your partner responds briefly.

Then the examiner gives your partner two different photographs. Your partner talks about these photographs for one minute. This time the examiner asks you a question about your partner's photographs and you respond briefly.

Part 3 (approximately 3 minutes)

The examiner asks you and your partner to talk together. You may be asked to solve a problem or try to come to a decision about something. For example, you might be asked to decide the best way to use some rooms in a language school. The examiner gives you a picture to help you but does not join in the conversation.

Part 4 (approximately 4 minutes)

The examiner joins in the conversation. You all talk together in a more general way about what has been said in Part 3. The examiner asks you questions but you and your partner are also expected to develop the conversation.

Test 4

PAPER 1   READING (1 hour 15 minutes)

Part 1

You are going to read a magazine article about a sport called paragliding. Choose the most suitable heading from the list **A-I** for each part (**1-7**) of the article. There is one extra heading which you do not need to use. There is an example at the beginning (**0**).

Mark your answers **on the separate answer sheet**.

A	Repetitive flights
B	Thoughts at the top of the mountain
C	Discovering the secret
D	A nervous landing
E	Floating above
F	Some personal attention
G	Heading for the take-off site
H	Obeying the command
I	An interest in a new sport

Fly like an Eagle

In the first report in our special feature on ACTIVITY HOLIDAYS WITH A DIFFERENCE, Anna Wootton takes to the air to experience the pleasures of paragliding.

0	I

A number of years ago, I'd seen bright-coloured wings in the air while on a skiing holiday in Chamonix, France. I soon found out what they were and how to go about learning this new mountain sport of 'paragliding'. When I went to live there a year later, I enrolled on the first available course at the local school.

1

The first of the five days of instruction is spent in a field learning the characteristics of the wing and everything which goes with it. Having spent some time untangling lines and preparing to take off, you are then ready to puff out the wing. You soon find out that forcing it does not work and that there is a technique to putting air into the cells, allowing the wing to rise above your head. This launch technique is practised again and again to teach you the importance of a clean take-off, as this is where the majority of accidents occur.

2

The following day is again spent practising blowing up the wing, but this time on a small hill. Applying the techniques, you take off and fly about 100 metres, then land gently below. Flying, landing, collecting the wing over your shoulder and walking back up the hill become exhausting, but eventually everything starts to come together. Your ability and confidence rise until you are informed that all the course students are ready to make their first major flight.

3

After a restless night, you rise to peer up at the mountain, knowing that today you are going to launch yourself off it. You feel sick as you take the lift up. With a dry mouth you mentally rehearse all that you've been taught. You don't want to admit it, but you're scared. However, you also know that you have got this far and there is no way that you are going to back out.

4

At 1,000 metres above the town, which now looks very small below, you certainly have doubts about why you are here. No-one in your group is pushing to go first; everyone takes their time laying out their wings and preparing to fly. Having checked and rechecked everything, you put your helmet on, switch on the radio and strap yourself in.

5

Your turn comes and your instructor does a final check that all the lines are in the correct positions. Then he calmly informs you that he will stand directly in front, with his back to the wind, and when everything is right he will count to three and you are to run directly at him.

6

'OK, on me, 1 … 2 … 3 … go!!!' This is the last instruction you hear with your feet still on the ground. You run forward, you feel the lines tighten and the pull of the wing as it rises above your head. You correct its balance and keep running off the side of the mountain. The wing lifts you and the mountain drops dramatically away.

7

On your first flight, you don't seem to get a chance to take in the view. You dare not move, but you do realise the expanse of air between you and the ground over 1,000 metres below. And everything is silent except for the wonderful sound of the air rushing through your helmet.

Part 2

You are going to read an article in which a film critic talks about his work. For questions **8-15**, choose the answer (**A**, **B**, **C** or **D**) which you think fits best according to the text.

Mark your answers **on the separate answer sheet**.

Film Critic

Mark Adams looks back over the last ten years of his work
as a film critic for a newspaper called *The Front Page*.

Writing articles about films for *The Front Page* was my first proper job. Before then I had done bits of reviewing – novels for other newspapers, films for a magazine and anything I was asked to do for the radio. That was how I met Tom Seaton, the first arts editor of *The Front Page*, who had also written for television. He hired me, but Tom was not primarily a journalist, or he would certainly have been more careful in choosing his staff.

At first, his idea was that a team of critics should take care of the art forms that didn't require specialised knowledge: books, TV, theatre, film and radio. There would be a weekly lunch at which we would make our choices from the artistic material that Tom had decided we should cover, though there would also be guests to make the atmosphere sociable.

It all felt like a bit of a dream at that time: a new newspaper, and I was one of the team. It seemed so unlikely that a paper could be introduced into a crowded market. It seemed just as likely that a millionaire wanted to help me personally, and was pretending to employ me. Such was my lack of self-confidence. In fact, the first time I saw someone reading the newspaper on the London underground, then turning to a page on which one of my reviews appeared, I didn't know where to look.

Tom's original scheme for a team of critics 31 for the arts never took off. It was a good idea, but we didn't get together as planned and so everything was done by phone. It turned out, too, that the general public out there preferred to associate a reviewer with a single subject area, and so I chose film. Without Tom's initial push, though, we would hardly have come up with the present arrangement, by which I write an extended weekly piece, usually on one film.

The luxury of this way of working suits me 40 well. I wouldn't have been interested in the more standard film critic's role, which involves considering every film that comes out. That's a routine that would make me stale in no time at all. I would soon be sinking into my seat on a Monday morning with the sigh, 'What insulting rubbish must I sit through now?' – a style of sigh that can often be heard in screening rooms around the world.

The space I am given allows me to broaden my argument – or forces me, in an uninteresting week, to make something out of nothing. But what is my role in the public arena? I assume that people choose what films to go to on the basis of the stars, the publicity or the director. There is also such a thing as loyalty to 'type' or its opposite. It can only rarely happen that someone who hates westerns buys a ticket for one after reading a review, or a love story addict avoids a romantic film because of what the papers say.

So if a film review isn't really a consumer guide, what is it? I certainly don't feel I have a responsibility to be 'right' about a movie. Nor do I think there should be a certain number of 'great' and 'bad' films each year. All I have to do is put forward an argument. I'm not a judge, and nor would I want to be.

8 What do we learn about Tom Seaton in the first paragraph?

    A He encouraged Mark to become a writer.

    B He has worked in various areas of the media.

    C He met Mark when working for television.

    D He prefers to employ people that he knows.

9 The weekly lunches were planned in order to

    A help the writers get to know each other.

    B provide an informal information session.

    C distribute the work that had to be done.

    D entertain important visitors from the arts.

10 When Mark first started working for *The Front Page*, he

    A doubted the paper would succeed.

    B was embarrassed at being recognised.

    C felt it needed some improvement.

    D was surprised to be earning so much.

11 What does Mark mean when he says that Tom's scheme 'never took off' (line 31)?

    A It was unpopular.

    B It wasted too much time.

    C It wasn't planned properly.

    D It wasn't put into practice.

12 In the end, the organisation of the team was influenced by

    A readers' opinions.

    B the availability of writers.

    C pressure of time.

    D the popularity of subjects.

13 Why does Mark refer to his way of working as a 'luxury' (line 40)?

    A He can please more readers.

    B He is able to make choices.

    C His working hours are flexible.

    D He is able to see a lot of films.

14 In Mark's opinion, his articles

    A are seldom read by filmgoers.

    B are ignored by stars and film directors.

    C have little effect on public viewing habits.

    D are more persuasive than people realise.

15 Which of the following best describes what Mark says about his work?

    A His success varies from year to year.

    B He prefers to write about films he likes.

    C He can freely express his opinion.

    D He writes according to accepted rules.

Part 3

You are going to read a newspaper article about a dentist. Eight sentences have been removed from the article. Choose from the sentences **A-I** the one which fits each gap (**16-22**). There is one extra sentence which you do not need to use. There is an example at the beginning (**0**).

Mark your answers **on the separate answer sheet**.

Fun at the Dentist's?

If you walk into W. Lloyd Jerome's dental surgery in Glasgow, you'll see bright paintings and a fashionable blue couch which patients sit on while he checks their teeth. Jerome says, ' **0** **I** That's because they're frightened.'

He has tried to create an environment where people are not afraid. ' **16** I find that's one of the things that people associate with pain. In fact, my philosophy is that dental treatment should take place in an atmosphere of relaxation, interest and, above all, enjoyment.'

Which is all highly shocking for anyone (most of us) who associates dental treatment with pain, or at the very least, formal, clinical visits. He says, ' **17** '

Virtual-reality headsets are one of his new relaxation techniques. ' **18** The headsets are used for the initial check-up, where the patient sits on the blue couch and watches an underwater film while I look at their teeth. Then the headset switches to a special camera, to give the patient a visual tour around their mouth.'

Another key point is that the surgery smells more like a perfume shop than a dentist's. Today there is the smell of orange. ' **19** Smell is very important. That dental smell of surgical spirit can get the heart racing in minutes if you're frightened of dentists.'

Known as Glasgow's most fashionable dentist, Jerome is keen to point out that he takes his work very seriously. ' **20** '

For example, Jerome uses a special instrument which sprays warm water on the teeth to clean them, rather than scraping them. ' **21** '

Five years ago, Jerome went to the United States to do research. ' **22** ' He sees his patient-centred attitude as the start of a gradual movement towards less formality in the conservative British dentistry profession.

At that moment, a patient arrives. Jerome rushes over, offers him a cup of tea (herbal or regular), asks him what video he'd like to watch and leads him gently towards the chair.

A One of the things I found out there was that when you make it easier for the patient, you make it easier for yourself.

B That's why I don't wear a white coat.

C If people are relaxed, entertained and correctly treated, they will forget such previous negative experiences.

D The relaxation techniques are important but the quality of the treatment is the most important thing.

E We were the first practice in Britain to introduce them.

F It feels a bit strange, but as long as people are relaxed, it's not painful.

G Now they look forward to their visits here.

H When people walk in, I want them to realise with all their senses that it's not like going to the dentist's.

I Fifty per cent of the population only go to the dentist when they're in pain.

Part 4

You are going to read a magazine article about theme parks in Britain. For questions **23-35**, choose from the theme parks (**A-E**). The theme parks may be chosen more than once. There is an example at the beginning (**0**).

Mark your answers **on the separate answer sheet**.

Of which theme parks are the following stated?

We had no previous experience of places like this.	**0**	B
Some of the children showed they were frightened on a certain ride.	**23**	
The children were all young enough to enjoy it.	**24**	
It was good that you could find somewhere to rest.	**25**	
It was more enjoyable than we had expected.	**26**	
The children disagreed about what was the most frightening ride.	**27**	
The surroundings are not particularly attractive.	**28**	
We didn't mind having to wait to go on the rides.	**29**	
The children wanted to stay longer than we did.	**30**	
One of the rides seemed to finish very quickly.	**31**	
We were glad that the children couldn't go on a certain ride.	**32**	
One of the children had a better time than we had expected.	**33**	
It makes a claim which is accurate.	**34**	
None of the rides would frighten young children very much.	**35**	

Visual materials for Paper 5

1A

1B

1E

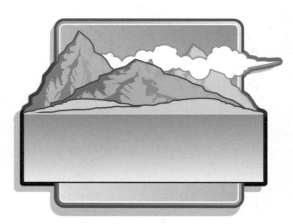

1C

1D

2A

2B

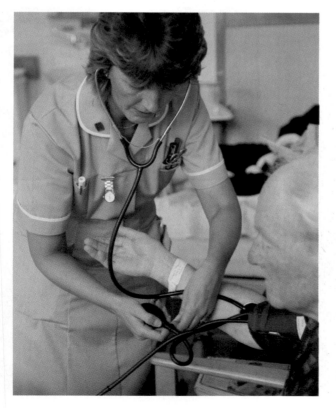

2C

2D

3A

3B

3E

3C

3D

4A

4B

4E

4C

4D

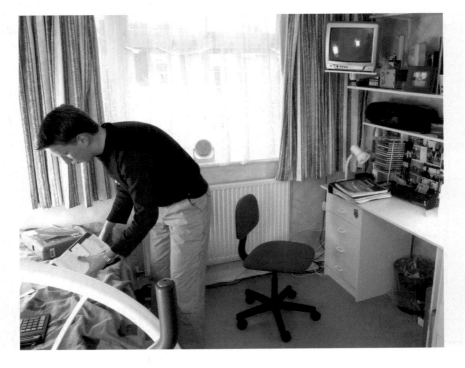

Variations on a Theme

If you're thinking of taking children to a theme park, there are dozens to choose from in Britain. We asked five families to test the best.

A Fun Island

Jan and Steve Burns took daughter Samantha, 3, and her cousins Gary, 8, and Jemma, 10.

Last year we went to a huge theme park in the US and we thought that Fun Island might seem dull by comparison. In fact, we were impressed. The park tries hard to cater for younger children, so our three-year-old didn't feel left out. The kids all loved the Crocodile Ride and the Giant Wheel. There's a special dodgems ride for the very young kids, which was a great success. For older children, there are scarier rides, such as Splash Out, where you end up jumping in a pool! After five hours, Steve and I were ready to call it a day, but the children objected because they were having such fun. Our only criticism would be that the park is slightly lacking in atmosphere, and the scenery leaves something to be desired. But the staff are extremely helpful and we felt it was clean, well organised and very security-conscious.

B Wonderland

Moira McMillan and her friend Frances took Oscar, 18 months, Ellie, 4, Alex, 5, and Alexander, 6.

None of us had been to a theme park before, so we didn't know what to expect. We thought Oscar might be too young, but he adored it. He was in heaven on the Mountain Train, and particularly liked Little Land, with its small replicas of famous buildings that were at his level! The older children enjoyed the ferris wheel, and loved driving the toy cars on a proper road layout. We spent six hours there and were glad that there were places where you could put your feet up. The landscaping is perfect and the staff very helpful and friendly. And there's something for everyone, adults included.

C Adventure World

Tim Jeffree and his wife Clare took Timothy, 3, Olivia, 7, and Emma, 9.

After seven hours we felt there was still a lot to see. This is an enormous theme park, extremely well run and full of good rides. The children love the Big Top Circus, which had a fantastic trapeze act and kept us on the edge of our seats. We went on the Terror Line and, although the girls were rather scared and kept their eyes shut most of the time, they said they'd enjoyed it. Their favourite ride was Running River, where you think you're going to get soaked, but you don't. For younger children, Toy Land is great fun. The children had a look at the new ride, Fear Factor, but we breathed a sigh of relief when they found that they were too small to go on it! The park is so well designed that even queuing for rides isn't too boring. It's spotlessly clean, and the staff are great. On one ride I couldn't sit with both girls, so a member of staff offered to go with one of them.

D The Great Park

Jenny Langridge and her friend Linda took Ben, 6, James, 9, and Sophie, 12.

We arrived at one o'clock and were disappointed that the park was only open until 5 p.m. This is a super theme park for younger children because the rides aren't too terrifying. I'm a real coward but even I enjoyed myself. We all adored Exotic Travels, a boat ride which starts off quite tamely and then becomes terrific fun. We queued for half an hour for Lightning River, and then it was over before we knew it! I wouldn't go on the Big Leap, but if you have the nerve, it looked great. There are lots of enjoyable boat and train trips around the park and I felt all the attractions were very safe and well controlled. If the children had been a little older, they might have found it a bit tame, but they were all in the right age group and they loved it.

E Fantasy World

Bill Breakall and his wife Ruth took Sarah, 10, Tom, 13, Jennie, 15, and Ben, 19.

According to the park's advertising there is 'No Limit to the Fun', and we certainly felt that was true. Europe's tallest roller-coaster, the Rocket, dominates the skyline, and Ben thought it was the most terrifying of the rides, although Jennie said the Hanger, where you hang upside-down 30 metres above the ground, was even worse! There are a dozen or so main rides, which the older children went on several times. Sarah was too small for a couple of them, but enjoyed the Long Slide. Tom loved the zoo and wildlife park. The park is clean and has good parking facilities. We found the staff attitudes were mixed. Some of them were great with the younger children, but the welcome wasn't always as warm. You need a full day to enjoy Fantasy World. We wouldn't have dared tell the kids we were going home early.

PAPER 2   WRITING (1 hour 30 minutes)

Part 1

You **must** answer this question.

1   Your English class is going to spend three days in London. The Principal of your college, Mr Robertson, has already organised the programme.

However, the students in your class have seen an advertisement for the *London Fashion and Leisure Show* and you would all like to go to the show. Your class has asked you to write to Mr Robertson about this. Read the extract from Mr Robertson's programme, the advertisement and your notes. Then, using the information, write a letter to Mr Robertson.

Monday 13 March
Morning: Sightseeing by bus
Afternoon: River trip to Greenwich

Tuesday 14 March
Morning: Science Museum
Afternoon: Shopping

Wednesday 15 March
Morning: National Art Gallery
Afternoon: Free time

THE LONDON FASHION AND LEISURE SHOW

Central Exhibition Hall, London
Tuesday March 14
10.00 – 19.00

- Latest fashions
- Leisure and sports wear
- Make-up
- Hairstyles

Students: free!

Notes

- *Thanks – good programme, especially …*
- *Explain about London Fashion and Leisure Show*
- *Great opportunity because …*
- *Suggest how programme could be changed*

Write a **letter** of between **120** and **180** words in an appropriate style on the opposite page. Do not write any postal addresses.

Question 1

....
....
....
....
....
....
....
....
....
....
....
....
....
....
....
....
....
....
....
....
....
....
....
....
....
....
....
....
....
....
....
....

Part 2

Write an answer to **one** of the questions **2-5** in this part. Write your answer in **120-180** words in an appropriate style on the opposite page. Put the question number in the box.

2 After a class discussion on the media's treatment of famous people, your teacher has asked you to write a composition, giving your opinions on the following statement:

Famous people, such as politicians and film stars, deserve to have a private life without journalists following them all the time.

Write your **composition**.

3 You see this announcement in an international magazine.

> We invite you, our readers, to write an article on:
>
> ### *The Home of the Future*
>
> In what ways do you think people's homes will be different in the future?
>
> In what ways might they still be the same?
>
> The writer of the best article will win a prize.

Write your **article**.

4 Your English teacher has asked you to write a story for the college magazine. Your story must **begin** with these words:

It was dangerous, but I knew I had to do it.

Write your **story**.

5 Answer **one** of the following two questions based on your reading of **one** of these set books. Write (**a**) or (**b**) as well as the number **5** in the question box, and the **title** of the book next to the box. Your answer **must** be about one of the books below.

Best Detective Stories of Agatha Christie – Longman Fiction
The Old Man and the Sea – Ernest Hemingway
A Window on the Universe – Oxford Bookworms Collection
Cry Freedom – John Briley
Wuthering Heights – Emily Brontë

Either (a) Your teacher has asked you to write a composition, giving your opinions on the following statement:

A good book should interest, amuse or teach the reader something.

Write your **composition**, explaining your views with reference to the book or one of the short stories you have read.

Or (b) Your pen friend has written to ask you whether the book you have read would be a suitable present for her cousin's fifteenth birthday. Write a letter to your pen friend, giving your opinion with reference to the book or short story you have read.

Write your **letter**.

Question [ ]

PAPER 3 USE OF ENGLISH (1 hour 15 minutes)

Part 1

For questions **1-15**, read the text below and decide which answer (**A**, **B**, **C** or **D**) best fits each space. There is an example at the beginning (**0**).

Mark your answers **on the separate answer sheet**.

Example:

0 A recommended   **B** reminded   **C** recognised   **D** remembered

0	A	B	C	D
	—	—	—	**—**

A FAMOUS EXPLORER

Captain James Cook is **(0)** ..... today for being one of Britain's most famous explorers of the 18th century. Cook was **(1)** ..... most other explorers of the same period as he did not come from a wealthy family and had to work hard to **(2)** ..... his position in life. He was lucky to be **(3)** ..... by his father's employer, who saw that he was a bright boy and paid for him to attend the village school. At sixteen, he started **(4)** ..... in a shop in a fishing village **(5)** ..... on the coast and this was a turning **(6)** ..... in his life. He developed an interest in the sea and eventually joined the Royal Navy **(7)** ..... to see more of the world.

Cook was **(8)** ..... by sailing, astronomy and the production of maps, and quickly became an expert **(9)** ..... these subjects. He was also one of the first people to **(10)** ..... that scurvy, an illness often suffered by sailors, could be prevented by careful **(11)** ..... to diet. It was during his **(12)** ..... to the Pacific Ocean that Cook made his historic landing in Australia and the **(13)** ..... discovery that New Zealand was two **(14)** ..... islands. He became a national hero and still **(15)** ..... one today.

1 **A** different   **B** contrary   **C** distinct   **D** unlike

2 **A** manage   **B** succeed   **C** achieve   **D** fulfil

3 **A** remarked   **B** viewed   **C** glanced   **D** noticed

4 **A** trade   **B** work   **C** career   **D** job

5 **A** held   **B** placed   **C** positioned   **D** situated

6 **A** moment   **B** instant   **C** point   **D** mark

7 **A** in view   **B** in order   **C** as   **D** due

8 **A** keen   **B** eager   **C** fascinated   **D** enthusiastic

9 **A** from   **B** over   **C** in   **D** for

10 **A** regard   **B** estimate   **C** catch   **D** realise

11 **A** attention   **B** organisation **C** observation   **D** treatment

12 **A** travel   **B** voyage   **C** excursion   **D** tour

13 **A** serious   **B** superior   **C** major   **D** leading

14 **A** shared   **B** particular   **C** common   **D** separate

15 **A** keeps   **B** stands   **C** maintains   **D** remains

Part 2

For questions **16-30**, read the text below and think of the word which best fits each space. Use only **one** word in each space. There is an example at the beginning (**0**). Write your answers **on the separate answer sheet**.

Example:

0	*one*

INDOOR CLIMBING

Rock climbing is (**0**) ...*one*... of the UK's fastest growing sports. Nowadays, however, it's not necessary to head to the hills when you decide to (**16**) .... it up as a hobby. Indoor climbing is a great way to discover whether or (**17**) .... you have a head for heights. Whatever you may have (**18**) .... told, size and strength aren't that important in climbing. Climbers just (**19**) .... to be fit, with a good sense of balance. Man-made climbing walls have footholds and handholds (**20**) .... different shapes and sizes. Beginners can choose walls with holds near to (**21**) .... other. More difficult routes up the wall will have small handholds quite (**22**) .... apart.

Climbers work in pairs. (**23**) .... one person climbs, the other one stays on the ground, giving out the rope. You (**24**) .... taught to move your hands and feet correctly, plus how to rest and balance (**25**) .... the way up. Once you've mastered all of (**26**) .... basic moves, you can go for longer climbs. The great thing about climbing is that you can (**27**) .... better quite quickly. Most sports centres will include the cost of hiring equipment (**28**) .... the admission price, (**29**) .... is usually between £4 and £6 per visit. It's natural to be scared at (**30**) .... , but soon you'll realise that you're quite safe!

Part 3

For questions **31-40**, complete the second sentence so that it has a similar meaning to the first sentence, using the word given. **Do not change the word given**. You must use between **two** and **five** words, including the word given.

Here is an example (**0**).

Example:

0   You must do exactly what the manager tells you.

carry

You must .... instructions exactly.

The gap can be filled by the words 'carry out the manager's' so you write:

0	*carry out the manager's*

Write **only the missing words** on the separate answer sheet.

---

31   My brother accused me of taking his car.

took

'You .... you?' said my brother.

32   That's the strangest film I've ever seen!

strange

I've .... film before!

33   A very friendly taxi driver drove us into town.

driven

We .... a very friendly taxi driver.

34   My aunt was determined to pay for our tickets.

insisted

My aunt .... for our tickets.

35 The manager failed to persuade Karen to take the job.

succeed

The manager .... Karen to take the job.

36 I'd rather you didn't use that red pen.

mind

Would .... that red pen?

37 I last saw Mark a year ago.

since

I have .... year.

38 John impressed his new boss by settling down to work quickly.

good

John .... his new boss by settling down to work
quickly.

39 Tony regrets lying to his teacher.

wishes

Tony .... his teacher the truth.

40 I found it difficult to follow the instructions.

trouble

I .... the instructions.

Part 4

For questions **41-55**, read the text below and look carefully at each line. Some of the lines are correct, and some have a word which should not be there.

If a line is correct, put a tick (✓) by the number **on the separate answer sheet**. If a line has a word which should **not** be there, write the word **on the separate answer sheet**. There are two examples at the beginning (**0** and **00**).

Examples:

0	✓
00	*too*

FINLAND

0	Finland is a country in the far north of Europe. Most of it is forest
00	and there are too about sixty thousand lakes there as well. It has a population
41	of some five million people, about a million of them who living in the capital
42	city, Helsinki. There are two official languages, Finnish and Swedish,
43	with about six per cent of the population being Swedish-speaking. Many
44	people think of Finland as for a very cold country where it is dark most of
45	all the time. In the long winter, temperatures are indeed very low and in some
46	parts there is very little daylight. However, in the summer it is often hot
47	and sunny, and it hardly just gets dark at all at night. One thing that Finland
48	is famous for is the sauna. A sauna is a kind of hot steam bath. You sit in
49	a room where steam is produced out and the temperature gets very high. You
50	then wash yourself or have a swim. Some people they even roll in the snow
51	in the winter! Finland is a very much keen sporting nation and over the years it
52	has had a number of champions in any winter sports such as ski-jumping and
53	ice hockey, as well as by producing some great Olympic athletes, especially in
54	long-distance running and the javelin. Other Finns who have been gained
55	international fame include the composer, Sibelius, and the architect and designer,
	Alvar Aalto.

Part 5

For questions **56-65**, read the text below. Use the word given in capitals at the end of each line to form a word that fits in the space in the same line. There is an example at the beginning (**0**). Write your answers **on the separate answer sheet**.

Example: | **0** | *shortly* |

RUNNING ROUND THE WORLD

John Shaw will **(0)** .*shortly*. be setting off on a 50,000 km run,   **SHORT**

which will make him the first person to perform the **(56)** ..... act   **ORDINARY**

of running all the way round the world if he succeeds.

His timetable includes the **(57)** ..... Russian winter and the burning   **FREEZE**

African summer. And he has no back-up team for **(58)** ..... . He will be   **ASSIST**

running alone, carrying all his **(59)** ..... on his back.   **EQUIP**

'My biggest fear is not the physical challenge, but **(60)** ..... ,' Mr Shaw   **LONELY**

said. 'I'm as sociable as anyone and I'm very **(61)** ..... that   **HOPE**

I will form many **(62)** ..... on the way.'   **FRIEND**

On a trial 2,000 km run under the blazing **(63)** ..... of the African sun,   **HOT**

he came across wild baboons and **(64)** ..... snakes, but he proved that   **POISON**

a target of 60 kilometres a day was **(65)** ..... . 'I have made up my   **REASON**

mind to do it and I will. Running is my life,' he said.

PAPER 4   LISTENING (approximately 40 minutes)

Part 1

You will hear people talking in eight different situations. For questions **1-8**, choose the best answer (**A**, **B** or **C**).

1   You overhear some people talking at a party in a hotel.
    Where did the people first meet each other?

    A   at school

    B   at work

    C   at a wedding

    | 1 |

2   You overhear a conversation in a restaurant.
    Why haven't they seen each other lately?

    A   He has been too busy.

    B   He has been ill.

    C   He has been away.

    | 2 |

3   You overhear someone talking about a concert.
    How did she feel at the time?

    A   angry

    B   frightened

    C   disappointed

    | 3 |

4   You hear a writer of children's stories talking about books
    and compact discs.
    What advantage does he think books have over compact discs?

    A   They may last for a longer time.

    B   They are easier to look after.

    C   They contain better quality material.

    | 4 |

5 You hear a husband and wife talking about their summer holidays.
What problem do they have?

    A   They really hate flying anywhere.

    B   They can never think of anywhere to go.

    C   They never agree about what to do.

        5

6 You hear a researcher being asked about her work.
What is she doing when she speaks?

    A   denying an accusation

    B   disproving a theory

    C   accepting a criticism

        6

7 You overhear a woman talking to a friend on a train.
What does the woman think of the course she has attended?

    A   It has made her feel more confident.

    B   It has made her feel less confident.

    C   It hasn't made much difference to how she feels.

        7

8 You overhear a woman speaking on the radio.
What is she doing?

    A   complaining about something

    B   apologising for something

    C   explaining something

        8

Part 2

You will hear a radio report about dolphins. For questions **9-18**, complete the sentences.

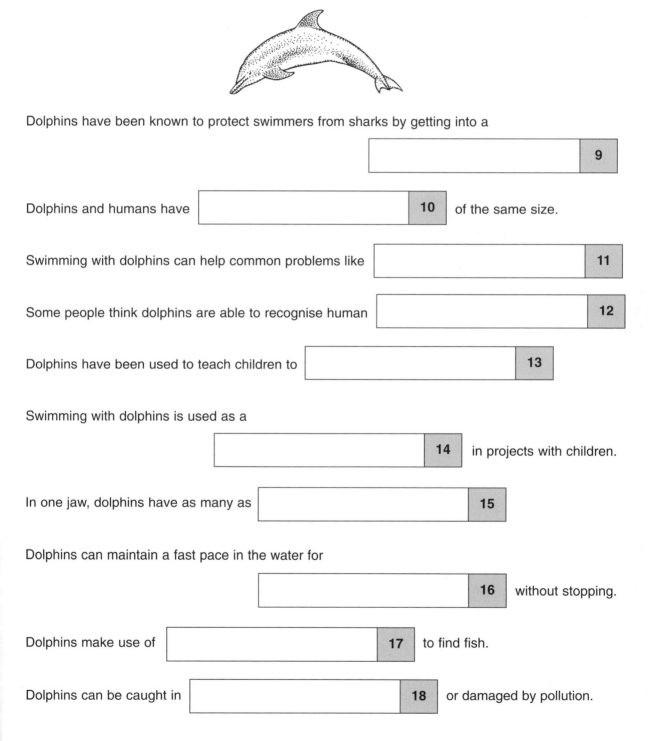

Dolphins have been known to protect swimmers from sharks by getting into a

	9

Dolphins and humans have | **10** | of the same size.

Swimming with dolphins can help common problems like | **11** |

Some people think dolphins are able to recognise human | **12** |

Dolphins have been used to teach children to | **13** |

Swimming with dolphins is used as a

| | **14** | in projects with children.

In one jaw, dolphins have as many as | **15** |

Dolphins can maintain a fast pace in the water for

| | **16** | without stopping.

Dolphins make use of | **17** | to find fish.

Dolphins can be caught in | **18** | or damaged by pollution.

Part 3

You will hear five different people talking about the head teacher or principal of their former secondary school. For questions **19-23**, choose from the list (**A-F**) what each speaker is saying. Use the letters only once. There is one extra letter which you do not need to use.

A She favoured the talented students.

| | Speaker 1 | | 19 |

B She prepared us for the real world.

| | Speaker 2 | | 20 |

C She encouraged us to be imaginative.

| | Speaker 3 | | 21 |

D She was ahead of her time.

| | Speaker 4 | | 22 |

E She was concerned about the environment.

| | Speaker 5 | | 23 |

F She encouraged competitiveness.

Part 4

You will hear an interview with a tour leader who works for an adventure company in Africa.
For questions **24-30**, choose the best answer (**A**, **B** or **C**).

24   Don says that most of his passengers
   A are not students.
   B are looking for jobs.
   C work in conservation.

     24

25   When Don first meets a group, he
   A gives them blankets for the overnight trip.
   B shows them where to sit on the truck.
   C checks they have the right equipment.

     25

26   Don remembers one trip when
   A he failed to take enough food.
   B someone made a mistake with the food.
   C someone complained about the food.

     26

27   Don oversees the domestic work because
   A he doesn't like to lose things.
   B it has to be done within an hour.
   C people complain if things are dirty.

     27

28   If people argue, Don says that he
   A prefers not to get involved.
   B separates the people concerned.
   C asks the group for a solution.

     28

29   Don says that he sometimes
   A needs to get to sleep early.
   B has to camp in a noisy area.
   C tells people when to go to bed.

     29

30   What does Don say about getting up?
   A He ignores any complaints about the time.
   B He varies his schedule according to the group.
   C He forces everyone to be quick about it.

     30

PAPER 5   SPEAKING (14 minutes)

You take the Speaking test with another candidate, referred to here as your partner. There are two examiners. One will speak to you and your partner and the other will be listening. Both examiners will award marks.

Part 1 (3 minutes)

The examiner asks you and your partner questions about yourselves. You may be asked about things like 'your home town', 'your interests', 'your career plans', etc.

Part 2 (4 minutes)

The examiner gives you two photographs and asks you to talk about them for one minute. The examiner then asks your partner a question about your photographs and your partner responds briefly.

Then the examiner gives your partner two different photographs. Your partner talks about these photographs for one minute. This time the examiner asks you a question about your partner's photographs and you respond briefly.

Part 3 (approximately 3 minutes)

The examiner asks you and your partner to talk together. You may be asked to solve a problem or try to come to a decision about something. For example, you might be asked to decide the best way to use some rooms in a language school. The examiner gives you a picture to help you but does not join in the conversation.

Part 4 (approximately 4 minutes)

The examiner joins in the conversation. You all talk together in a more general way about what has been said in Part 3. The examiner asks you questions but you and your partner are also expected to develop the conversation.

Test 1 Key

Paper 1　Reading (1 hour 15 minutes)

Part 1

1 F　　2 D　　3 B　　4 H　　5 G　　6 A　　7 E

Part 2

8 A　　9 C　　10 D　　11 B　　12 B　　13 C　　14 D

Part 3

15 C　　16 G　　17 E　　18 H　　19 B　　20 A　　21 F

Part 4

22 C　　23 B　　24 A　　25/26 A/B (*in either order*)　　27 B
28/29 C/D (*in either order*)　　30/31 B/C (*in either order*)
32/33 A/C (*in either order*)　　34/35 C/E (*in either order*)

Paper 2　Writing (1 hour 30 minutes)

Task-specific mark schemes

Part 1

Question 1
Content
Major points: The letter must include the following points.
1) the pen and pencil are not very attractive
2) the name is misspelt
3) the pen and pencil do not match
4) the gift arrived too late
5) the writer must ask for their money back

Organisation and cohesion
Letter format, with early reference to why the person is writing. Suitable paragraphing. Clear organisation of points. Suitable opening and closing formulae.

Appropriacy of register and format
Formal letter.

Range
Language of complaint, explanation and request.

Target reader
Would understand the nature and detail of the complaint and would have enough information to consider the request for a refund.

Part 2

Question 2

Content

Composition could agree or disagree with the proposition, or discuss both sides of the argument.

Range

Language of opinion, explanation and description. Vocabulary relevant to clothes.

Organisation and cohesion

Clear development of viewpoint with appropriate paragraphing and linking of ideas.

Appropriacy of register and format

Neutral composition.

Target reader

Would be able to understand the writer's viewpoint.

Question 3

Content

Article should suggest one of the four ideas given for a club and state why the writer is choosing that idea. There should also be one other idea (either from the list or the writer's own idea), with the reason for suggesting that idea.

Range

Language of suggestion and explanation.

Organisation and cohesion

Clear development of ideas, with appropriate linking and paragraphing.

Appropriacy of register and format

Register could range from the informal to the formal, but must be consistent throughout.

Target reader

Would know which clubs the writer would like to see started after school and why.

Question 4

Content

Report should give factual information about things for visitors to see and do in the writer's area in one day (acceptable to mention just one thing).

Range

Language appropriate to giving information and making suggestions.

Organisation and cohesion

Report should be clearly organised. Sub-headings would be an advantage, if not, suitable paragraphing. There should be an introduction and a conclusion.

Appropriacy of register and format
Formal report layout is not essential. Register could range from the neutral
to the formal, but must be consistent throughout.

Target reader
Would know what to do in the writer's area in one day.

Question 5(a)
Content
Writer can agree or disagree with the proposition that the characters are
believable and should explain their opinion with reference to the book or
short story read.

Range
Language of opinion and explanation.

Organisation and cohesion
Clear development of viewpoint with appropriate paragraphing and linking
of ideas.

Appropriacy of register and format
Neutral composition.

Target reader
Would be able to understand the writer's point of view.

Question 5(b)
Content
Letter should give information about the book or short story/stories and state
whether the writer would recommend it or not to their friend to read. The writer
should also give reasons for their recommendation or lack of recommendation.

Range
Language of narration, description and explanation.

Organisation and cohesion
Letter format, with early reference to why the person is writing. Clear organisation
of points. Suitable opening and closing formulae. Appropriate paragraphing.

Appropriacy of register and format
Informal letter.

Target reader
Would be informed about the book or short story/stories and would know
whether it would be a good choice to read and why.

Paper 3   Use of English (1 hour 15 minutes)

Part 1

1 A	2 D	3 B	4 C	5 B	6 C	7 A	8 C
9 D	10 B	11 B	12 C	13 C	14 B	15 B	

Part 2

16 where   17 when/while   18 with   19 and   20 so   21 as
22 would   23 something   24 for   25 without/avoiding
26 having/facing/experiencing   27 up   28 a   29 since/because/as
30 had

Part 3

31 in **order** | to be
32 is | no **point**
33 **until** | we had finished/done
34 was **better** | than Tim
35 if | she **does** not do OR unless | she **does**
36 if/whether he realised | **what** time
37 **put** an advertisement | for
38 **finished** his speech | before thanking OR **finished** (his speech) | by thanking
39 has been / is | a **month** since
40 **following** their | appearance

Part 4

41 been   42 which   43 ✓   44 hardly   45 ✓   46 had
47 have   48 ✓   49 last   50 extra   51 out   52 those
53 ✓   54 myself   55 because

Part 5

56 variety   57 director   58 inhabitants   59 choice/choices
60 growth   61 unemployment   62 agreement   63 loss
64 unable   65 decision

Test 1

Paper 4   Listening (40 minutes approximately)

Part 1

1 A   2 A   3 C   4 B   5 C   6 B   7 C   8 A

Part 2

9 graves   10 twelfth century   11 their/the owners
12 make(-)up   13 ten thousand pounds
14 original clothes   15 soft bodies
16 maker(')s name(s)   17 (little) adults   18 plastic

Part 3

19 E   20 F   21 D   22 B   23 C

Part 4

24 J   25 TT   26 J   27 J   28 TT   29 A   30 J

First Certificate in English 6 (CUP)
ISBN: 0-521-75445-3

Transcript   *First Certificate Listening Test. Test One.*
Hello. I'm going to give you the instructions for this test. I'll introduce each part of the test and give you time to look at the questions. At the start of each piece you'll hear this sound:

tone

You'll hear each piece twice.

Remember, while you're listening, write your answers on the question paper. You'll have time at the end of the test to copy your answers onto the separate answer sheet.

There will now be a pause. Please ask any questions now, because you must not speak during the test.

[pause]

Now open your question paper and look at Part One.

[pause]

PART 1   *You'll hear people talking in eight different situations. For questions 1 to 8, choose the best answer, A, B or C.*

Question 1   *One.*
You hear part of a radio play.
Where is the scene taking place?
A   in the street
B   in a bank
C   in a police station

[pause]

tone

Policeman: So what happened, madam?
Woman: Well, I saw this old man, he was kind of holding this briefcase under his arm, like this. He'd just left the bank and I was still queuing up to collect my pension, but I was near that door. Now, this young man came running past him and grabbed him by the arm.
Policeman: And they both fell down?
Woman: Yeah, and the young man ran away and the poor old man sat on the pavement, still clutching his briefcase, and we managed to help him up. Now, can I go back in to collect my money?
Policeman: Would you mind coming with us, madam? We need a few more details.

[pause]

tone

[The recording is repeated.]

[pause]

Question 2   *Two.*
You overhear the beginning of a lecture.
What subject are the students taking?
A   medicine
B   sport
C   music

[pause]

tone

Woman: It's important that you really listen to what people are telling you. For example, I had a trumpet player who came to see me with back pain and breathing difficulties. He couldn't take his final exams because of the muscular tension in his jaw, but when I quizzed him about it, it turned out that the actual problem was in his teeth – far away from where the pain actually was. The same applies to sports people who often have injuries as a result of their job …

[pause]

tone

[The recording is repeated.]

[pause]

Question 3   *Three.*
You overhear a conversation in a college.
Who is the young man?
A   a new student
B   a student in the middle of a course
C   a former student

[pause]

tone

Man: It all looks so different. Where's the canteen?
Woman: It's in the basement. You get there by going down the main staircase from the entrance hall.
Man: Right. I'll get there in the end. Everything seems to have moved around.
Woman: Yes, there was a re-building programme last year, which wasn't much fun for those of us trying to study. The main building was altered a lot. And they're building a new sports centre. It should be open for the new students in September.
Man: Well, I'm envious. Everything looks a lot better.

[pause]

tone

[The recording is repeated.]

[pause]

Question 4	Four. *You hear a woman on the radio talking about a cookbook.* *What does she regret?* A *not looking after it* B *not having kept it* C *not using it properly*

[pause]

tone

Woman:	I used to watch granny cooking, and right from when I was five years old, I was allowed to season the soups, test the potatoes and so on. One year for my birthday, she bought me a cookbook. It was just like granny talking; all the recipes were simple, economical and linked with little stories, useful advice and amusing sketches. I treasured it, but gradually it fell to bits from overuse, my tastes changed and, finally, I threw it out. Now, of course, I wish I'd hung on to it despite its sad state and despite the fact that all the advice would be out of date.

[pause]

tone

[The recording is repeated.]

[pause]

Question 5	Five. *You hear someone talking about the day he met someone famous.* *How did he feel after meeting Chris Turner?* A *unimpressed with the footballer* B *angry with his friend* C *disappointed with himself*

[pause]

tone

Man:	I went to a party with a friend and she knows that I'm a big fan of Chris Turner, the footballer. I just think he's a genius and, anyway he was going to be there. Now, I knew that I would be really shy, which is stupid because he's exactly the same age as me and, you know, he's just a regular bloke, I'm sure. But when my friend introduced us and he shook my hand, my mouth just went, you know, really dry and I didn't know what to say, honestly, which was awful. I felt so bad about it afterwards, my friend just couldn't understand it.

[pause]

tone

[The recording is repeated.]

[pause]

Question 6   *Six.*
              You hear a woman talking on the phone.
              Why has she called?
              A   to request a meeting
              B   to offer assistance
              C   to apologise for her absence

              [pause]

              tone

Woman: Hi, can I just talk to you about our plans for the Summer Conference? I think I
              said that I was going to be away for the opening meeting and couldn't give you a
              hand, but it seems I got my diary muddled up and I will actually be around, so
              what would you like me to do?

              [pause]

              tone

              [The recording is repeated.]

              [pause]

Question 7   *Seven.*
              You overhear an extract from a radio play.
              What is the young woman's relationship with the man?
              A   She's a pupil of his.
              B   She's a relative of his.
              C   She's a patient of his.

              [pause]

              tone

Man: So, Sophie, tell me all about it.
Woman: I'm sorry, but I've just been feeling terrible for the last week or so and last night I
              just couldn't do my homework, I felt so bad. I was aching all over. So my Dad
              said I had better make an appointment and come and see you. Perhaps you can
              tell me what's wrong.

              [pause]

              tone

              [The recording is repeated.]

              [pause]

Question 8   *Eight.*
              You hear someone telling a story about a strange thing that happened in the
              mountains.
              What point does the story prove?
              A   how strange things can be explained simply
              B   how easy it is to imagine things
              C   how you can be tricked by the silence

[pause]

tone

Man: My wife Margaret and I were sitting behind a rock on the top of a mountain in the Highlands one day, nobody else around, perfectly silent, and Margaret said, 'I just heard a telephone bell ringing.' 'Oh,' I said, 'Margaret, there are no telephone kiosks up here.' But in the silence of the hills, you can imagine anything. I said, 'I often imagine things. I've heard babies crying in this silence. I've thought I heard a symphony orchestra,' and Margaret said, 'I'm sure I heard a telephone ringing.' She got up and went round the back of the rock and there was a cow with a bell around its neck.

[pause]

tone

[The recording is repeated.]

[pause]

That's the end of Part One.

Now turn to Part Two.

[pause]

PART 2   *You'll hear part of a talk about dolls. For questions 9 to 18 complete the sentences.*

   You now have forty-five seconds in which to look at Part Two.

[Pause the recording here for 45 seconds.]

tone

Man: Dolls have always fascinated me, and that's why, five years ago, I was delighted to be offered the job of running a doll museum.

   Dolls have existed for thousands of years, and the earliest dolls we know about were found in graves in ancient Egypt. I only wish we could get one or two for our museum, but we haven't unfortunately, got anything as old as that in the museum. All the same, we have got examples from Europe from the twelfth century, but my favourite early dolls are actually from the seventeenth century. They interest me not just because they are early, or fairly early, but also because of the clothes they're wearing. They have their original clothes, and from them we know what the owners wore, since dolls in those days were always dressed like their owners. They were made of the only material readily available for things like this at the time: solid wood, and they were painted in great detail. In fact, on the best examples, like the ones in the museum, the detail includes the seventeenth century make-up.

   Dolls like these were very expensive then, and only the very rich could afford them. These days, they're popular with collectors and if you want one today, you have to pay anything up to £10,000 for a doll in perfect condition from this time! By the way, what makes them so valuable is that, as far as a collector is concerned, a doll is only worth collecting if it is in perfect condition, and that means having the original clothes.

Doll collecting has become very fashionable since the museum opened, with people interested in dolls from every period, including later dolls. There's great interest in nineteenth century examples, when dolls were no longer made of wood, but began to have soft bodies and real hair. They were very delicate and few have survived, meaning such a doll would be worth about £2000, perhaps a bit more. Later, in the nineteenth century, you could often take off the doll's hair. If you can, you can often see the maker's name underneath, and of course the right one increases a doll's value.

There was a really big change in dolls at the beginning of the twentieth century. In the museum we have one of the earliest examples, from about 1909, of a doll that's a model of a baby. Previously all dolls, the earlier ones, were little adults. That's just one of the changes that have occurred in the last hundred years. Another, again, is to do with what dolls are made of. Although dolls with soft bodies continued, after about 1930, plastic began to be used. In fact, dolls from the 1930s and 40s are now very popular with collectors, some of them selling for very, very high prices.

[pause]

Now you'll hear Part Two again.

tone

[The recording is repeated.]

[pause]

That's the end of Part Two.

Now turn to Part Three.

[pause]

PART 3   *You'll hear five different people talking about why they decided to become nurses. For questions 19 to 23, choose which of the reasons A to F each speaker is giving. Use the letters only once. There's one extra letter which you do not need to use.*

You now have thirty seconds in which to look at Part Three.

[Pause the recording here for 30 seconds.]

tone

Speaker 1

[pause]

Well I have to say, I never really thought about a career until I got to my last year at school. Lots of people here say that they knew exactly what they wanted to do right from a very young age, but I never really had any burning ambitions. In the end I just sort of drifted into it because that's what our lot have always done. If I'd chosen something else – like going into business, say – I would have been the first for four generations to have gone outside the medical field. I don't think that that would have mattered but it means there are lots of things we can talk about at home.

[pause]

Speaker 2

[pause]

Most of my friends went into teaching actually – I think they felt it was more 'academic' and of course the pay is quite a bit better. But I've never really been bothered about things like that – I think the enjoyment of the job comes first and I certainly get a lot of good feelings doing this work. We have some difficult cases sometimes but there's still a lot of laughter here and the patients can be amazing – especially the kids. I'd recommend it to anyone who likes helping people.

[pause]

Speaker 3

[pause]

I think I'm lucky really because I didn't try very hard at school – I guess you'd call me lazy! And then it ended and I thought 'Wow, I'd better think about a job,' and I got really worried and emotional about it because, well, I suddenly realised that I didn't want to go from job to job, you know. I wanted a career and regular money and an opportunity to climb up the ladder if possible. So, one day I saw a TV programme about nursing and it looked like it had the kind of benefits that I wanted – so here I am.

[pause]

Speaker 4

[pause]

At first I thought I'd made the wrong choice … you know, I was never really sure that it was the thing for me and I used to go back to my flat at night and think – well maybe I should have listened to my parents after all. They thought I'd get too upset and that I should have stuck with something office-based like the rest of my family but it was my best subject at school – well Biology was – and all the staff there thought medicine would be a good choice, so … Anyway, one day I woke up and felt fine about it and it's been great ever since.

[pause]

Speaker 5

[pause]

I remember we all had to go to this Careers Advisor in our last year at school and I think she got really confused when she saw me because I just had no idea. I liked the sound of a lot of jobs and I couldn't make up my mind. When the time came to tell our teachers what we were going to apply for, I thought – well what *does* matter to me is being separate from my friends and so I went round to see one of them – the most important I suppose, and anyway she had chosen nursing, so that was it really – a difficult decision made easy, although I must say, I've never regretted it.

[pause]

Now you'll hear Part Three again.

tone

[The recording is repeated.]

[pause]

That's the end of Part Three.

Now turn to Part Four.

[pause]

PART 4   *You'll hear part of a radio programme in which a book critic gives information about three new books on the subject of travelling in the United States of America. For questions 24 to 30, decide which book each statement refers to. Write A for A TO Z, J for JUST GO or TT for TRAVEL TREAT.*

You now have forty-five seconds in which to look at Part Four.

[Pause the recording here for 45 seconds.]

tone

Critic: Well, this week we have three new travel guides about the USA, *A to Z to the USA* by Peter Tongue, *Just Go* by Carol Brand and *Travel Treat* by John Barnes. Travel guides should give us not just all the practical details, but also background information, and *Just Go* manages to pack in more of the latest developments in public life, civic affairs and government than the usual guide. For some reason, *Travel Treat* and *A to Z* tend to ignore this. Though it must be said that *Travel Treat* does give you a good insight into the American way of life.

 With travel guides I tend to feel that the writer's experience is crucial. Now, these three writers are young, but when you read *A to Z*, what strikes you is that the author is a sophisticated world traveller who has clocked amazing mileage throughout thirty countries and four continents.

 Nevertheless, there's a feeling that this time he has not put in as much work prior to writing. And you have the same impression with *Just Go*. *Travel Treat*, on the other hand, seems to be based on an incredible amount of serious work, although the author is not nearly as widely travelled.

 Some travel guide books manage to take travellers away from the tourist trail, and *Just Go* is outstanding in this respect, with extensive coverage of areas which other guides don't think worth mentioning. To be fair, *A to Z* also tries to encourage you to depart from the beaten track, but it doesn't succeed quite as well.

 Travel Treat can at times be a bit on the dull side, while *Just Go* tries to be funny without really succeeding. *A to Z*, however, is one of those books where, although I'm sure it wasn't the author's intention that we should laugh, you just can't help seeing the funny side of some of the misfortunes of this enthusiastic traveller!

 All the guides give good advice on health. In *Just Go* and *A to Z*, you are told what to do about drugs, the heat … all the important details. In addition to that, *Travel Treat* also tells you about the kind of medical insurance you need to take out before you go.

Well, next, I think all three travel guides make a real effort to provide tips about where to go for entertainment. *A to Z* is particularly good for people travelling on a tight budget because it tells you how to avoid all the tourist traps ... and still see the best shows in town. *Just Go* tends to concentrate more on the upmarket end of the scale, and so does *Travel Treat*, although both of them have some very good advice.

And finally, I think from this point of view, *Just Go* gives the reader the whole range of options, from staying with families to luxury hotels for those who can afford it. *A to Z* and *Travel Treat* are not as comprehensive, but they both have a very good section on activity holidays, staying on farms or ranches.

[pause]

Now you'll hear Part Four again.

tone

[The recording is repeated.]

[pause]

That's the end of Part Four.

There'll now be a pause of five minutes for you to copy your answers onto the separate answer sheet.

[Pause the recording here for five minutes. Remind your students when they have one minute left.]

That's the end of the test. Please stop now. Your supervisor will now collect all the question papers and answer sheets.

Goodbye.

Test 2 Key

Paper 1   Reading (1 hour 15 minutes)

Part 1

1 G   2 E   3 B   4 H   5 F   6 A   7 D

Part 2

8 B   9 B   10 D   11 C   12 A   13 A   14 D   15 C

Part 3

16 F   17 A   18 C   19 G   20 D   21 E

Part 4

22 D   23 A   24 D   25/26 C/E (*in either order*)   27 B   28 E
29/30 A/B (*in either order*)   31 C   32/33 B/D (*in either order*)   34 C
35 D

Paper 2   Writing (1 hour 30 minutes)

Task-specific mark schemes

Part 1

Question 1

Content
Major points: Letter must include all the points in the notes.
1) commenting on the choice of hotel
2) suggesting food for the party
3) explaining why a watch is not a good idea for a present and/or suggesting something else
4) apologising for not being able to help the day before
5) suggesting something else for the party

Organisation and cohesion
Letter format, with early reference to why the person is writing. Clear organisation of points. Suitable opening and closing formulae.

Appropriacy of register and format
Informal letter.

Range
Language appropriate for making suggestions, giving reasons and apologising.

Target reader
Would be informed about the writer's ideas for the party.

Part 2

Question 2

Content
Composition could agree or disagree with the proposition, or discuss both sides of the argument.

Range
Language of opinion and explanation. Vocabulary relevant to transport.

Organisation and cohesion
Clear development of viewpoint with appropriate paragraphing and linking of ideas.

Appropriacy of register and format
Neutral composition.

Target reader
Would be able to understand the writer's point of view.

Question 3

Content
Letter should explain why the writer is a suitable person for the job.

Range
Language of explanation, giving information and personal description.

Organisation and cohesion
Clear presentation and organisation in the letter. Suitable opening and closing formulae.

Appropriacy of register and format
Formal or semi-formal letter.

Target reader
Would have enough information to assess writer's suitability for the job.

Question 4

Content
Story should end with the prompt sentence.

Range
Past tenses. Vocabulary appropriate to the chosen topic for the story.

Organisation and cohesion
Could be minimally paragraphed. Should reach a definite ending, even if that ending is somewhat open-ended, as in many modern short stories.

Appropriacy of register and format
Consistent neutral or informal narrative.

Target reader
Would be able to follow the storyline.

Question 5(a)

Content
Composition should discuss the importance of the title of the book or short story and why the writer chose that title.

Range
Language of narration, description and explanation.

Organisation and cohesion
Clear development of ideas, with appropriate linking and paragraphing.

Appropriacy of register and format
Neutral composition.

Target reader
Would be informed about the importance of the title of the book or short story and why the author chose that title.

Question 5(b)

Content
Report on book or short story, either recommending it or not recommending it for members of the English book club.

Range
Language of giving information, description, narration and perhaps recommendation.

Organisation and cohesion
Report should be clearly organised. Sub-headings would be an advantage. There should be an introduction and a conclusion.

Appropriacy of register and format
Register could range from formal to informal, but must be consistent throughout. Formal report layout is not essential.

Target reader
Would be informed about the book or short story and whether the book is suitable to include on the list or not.

Paper 3 Use of English (1 hour 15 minutes)

Part 1

1 C   2 B   3 D   4 C   5 B   6 D   7 B   8 A
9 B   10 D   11 A   12 A   13 D   14 C   15 C

Part 2

16 because   17 more   18 of   19 are   20 too
21 be/sound   22 when/while/as   23 which   24 had/needed
25 what   26 again   27 would   28 if/provided   29 first
30 by

Part 3

31 would **like** | to know
32 **let** us | park (our car)
33 if | I had **seen**
34 **there** is | a hole in
35 was **called** | off
36 pays (any/much) **attention** | to
37 if she | would **lend** him OR to | **lend** him
38 **might** have | forgotten
39 **efficient** at | checking
40 (single) child | has (great) **fun**

Part 4

41 for   42 ✓   43 much   44 if   45 ✓   46 own   47 to
48 that   49 eat   50 the   51 ✓   52 ✓   53 at   54 it   55 ✓

Part 5

56 frequently   57 impressive   58 comfortable   59 flight(s)
60 communications   61 increasingly   62 improvement(s)
63 noisy   64 Crowded/Overcrowded   65 unfortunately

Paper 4   Listening (40 minutes approximately)

Part 1

1 A   2 A   3 C   4 B   5 A   6 B   7 C   8 C

Part 2

9 March   10 design   11 publicity
12 (in) (the) (two) meeting(s) rooms   13 £35   14 teachers
15 adults   16 acting   17 Ewington CORRECT SPELLING ONLY
18 (the) Education Manager

Part 3

19 F   20 B   21 A   22 E   23 C

Part 4

24 B   25 C   26 A   27 A   28 C   29 B   30 C

Transcript   *First Certificate Listening Test. Test Two.*
Hello. I'm going to give you the instructions for this test. I'll introduce
each part of the test and give you time to look at the questions. At the start
of each piece you'll hear this sound:

tone

You'll hear each piece twice.

Remember, while you're listening, write your answers on the question
paper. You'll have time at the end of the test to copy your answers onto
the separate answer sheet.

There will now be a pause. Please ask any questions now, because you
must not speak during the test.

[pause]

PART 1   *Now open your question paper and look at Part One.*

[pause]

You'll hear people talking in eight different situations. For questions 1 to
8, choose the best answer, A, B or C.

Question 1   *One.*
You overhear two people talking in a restaurant.
Where has the woman just come from?
A   *a supermarket*
B   *a hospital*
C   *a football match*

[pause]

tone

Woman: I felt so sorry for her, she just couldn't cope. She had the baby under one arm
and a list in the other. And he was screaming, all red in the face. She must have
only just come out of hospital, he was so tiny.
Man: So you offered to help.
Woman: Well, I wanted to get through the check-out and pay for my things quickly,
otherwise I knew I'd be late getting here, but …
Man: Well, I've only been here half an hour.
Woman: Oh, I'm sorry, there was such a queue. And then I forgot, it's the big football
game today and the roads were just packed …

[pause]

tone

[The recording is repeated.]

[pause]

Question 2   Two.
You hear a man talking about a mobile phone he has bought.
What most attracted him to this phone?
A   *its size*
B   *its reliability*
C   *its price*

[pause]

tone

Man: I've never wanted to walk around with an enormous mobile, you know, fixed to my belt or whatever, because that's socially embarrassing, isn't it? So I was really taken with the Edmundsen GP 876 model which you can just slip in your inside pocket and no one's the wiser, if you know what I mean. And it says in the blurb 'satisfaction guaranteed – should your mobile develop a fault in the first year, we will replace it the next day'. Well, to be honest, it wasn't exactly what you call cheap, so I'm rather hoping that I don't need to find out just how good that particular promise is.

[pause]

tone

[The recording is repeated.]

[pause]

Question 3   Three.
You hear a man talking on the phone about buying a house.
What is the purpose of his call?
A   *to apologise*
B   *to complain*
C   *to obtain information*

[pause]

tone

Man: Hello, it's Mr Brown here. I got your message. Yes, I was really sorry to hear the house I wanted had just been sold … Yes … I missed the chance to buy the house of my dreams. Yes, I know it wasn't your fault. I should have contacted you earlier. … Yes … That's why I'm now eager to hear of any houses that come on the market. As you know, what I want is a house which combines a kitchen and breakfast room with lots of space for living, eating and cooking. … Yes, I'm tired of small places where you can hardly move.

[pause]

tone

[The recording is repeated.]

[pause]

Question 4	*Four.*
	You hear a teenage girl talking about her hobby.
	What is she talking about?
	A a computer game
	B a musical instrument
	C a piece of sports equipment

[pause]

tone

Girl: I got it as a present from my father when I was fourteen. My family thought it would be a phase, that I'd go off the idea. Mum doesn't believe there'll be any money in it, but Dad is quite interested because, apart from football, it's the only thing I can talk to him about at the moment. If you're not going to make the effort to practise on it, no way is anyone going to be interested in you. I think one of the reasons you see so few girls playing in bands is that they tend not to be willing to do all that work.

[pause]

tone

[The recording is repeated.]

[pause]

Question 5	*Five.*
	On the news, you hear a story about a cat.
	Where was the cat found?
	A in a train carriage
	B on the railway lines
	C on a station platform

[pause]

tone

Newsreader: A cat with a mind of its own joined the 11.55 train from King's Lynn yesterday. A passenger spotted the cat, thought to have boarded at Littleport, and handed it to a member of the platform staff once the train got to Ely station. The friendly cat was put in a box and returned to Littleport. Eventually, its owner, Jack Prince, from Littleport, was reunited with his cat. It is thought that the cat must have crossed the lines at Littleport and waited on the platform, together with a dozen passengers who didn't notice it at all.

[pause]

tone

[The recording is repeated.]

[pause]

Question 6	*Six.*
	You hear a woman talking about how she gets ideas for her work.

124

Who is the woman?
A a novelist
B an artist
C a film-maker

[pause]

tone

Woman: I work with my husband, Bob, and every time we have a holiday somewhere, we seem to come up with an idea. And touring round the USA last year, he'd written the words for this children's ghost story. But I had no idea how to … to get the atmosphere in the pictures, which is my role in the partnership. And then we went to Las Vegas and all that amazing architecture, lit up at night under the desert sky, was er … was dreamlike. I mean, despite all the films, nothing prepares you for what it actually feels like to be there. I just sat down and started sketching out ideas on the spot.

[pause]

tone

[The recording is repeated.]

[pause]

Question 7   *Seven.*
You hear two people talking.
How does the woman feel?
A surprised
B satisfied
C relieved

[pause]

tone

Woman: There they are! At last. I've been looking for them everywhere.
Man: What? Your keys? You're always losing them.
Woman: I know, and I really thought I'd lost them for good this time. Thank goodness!
Man: Why don't you make sure you put them down in the same place, then you'd have the satisfaction of finding them whenever you wanted them.
Woman: Maybe. That's not a bad idea. I'll think about it.

[pause]

tone

[The recording is repeated.]

[pause]

Question 8   *Eight.*
You turn on the radio and hear a man speaking.
What are you listening to?

125

A   *a history programme*
B   *a science-fiction story*
C   *an advertisement*

[pause]

tone

Man: Discover the amazing secrets of the planet Earth in three major recently launched exhibitions: 'From the Beginning', 'Earth's Treasury' and 'Earth Today and Tomorrow' which form the finest series of exhibitions of their kind in the world. Together they tell Earth's dramatic story, starting with the birth of the universe, exploring the forces that shape it and the riches within it, concluding with a glimpse into the future and what it might hold for our planet.

[pause]

tone

[The recording is repeated.]

[pause]

That's the end of Part One.

Now turn to Part Two.

[Pause the recording here for 30 seconds.]

PART 2   *You will hear a radio interview with a woman who is organising a training weekend for people interested in the theatre. For questions 9 to 18, complete the notes.*

You now have forty-five seconds in which to look at Part Two.

[Pause the recording here for 45 seconds.]

tone

Interviewer: If you've ever dreamt of directing a play or designing a stage set, well the opportunity has arisen for you and who knows where it could lead. My next guest, Claire Ewington, from the local theatre, is here to tell us more about a practical weekend training event to start your dreams rolling, you might say. Good afternoon, Claire.
Claire: Good afternoon.
Interviewer: So, when is the training weekend and what does it involve?
Claire: It's the first weekend in March and there are two days of activities with a choice of activities on each day. The Saturday is either 'Design', which means a whole day working with a professional designer, or 'Directing' with a professional director and they'll be looking at the day to day workings of each of the professions with a chance to get involved. The same on Sunday, a full day of activities again, 'Make-up' or 'Press and publicity' are the choices.
Interviewer: And where will the course be taking place?
Claire: Well, each group will spend some time working on the stage, but actually we spend most of the time in two meeting rooms at the theatre. We can take up to 25 in either group on either day, so that's a total of 50 people each day.

Interviewer:	Okay. And how long does it last, each session?
Claire:	Each session is ten till five, with lunch breaks and coffee breaks included.
Interviewer:	How much does a weekend training event cost?
Claire:	For the participants it's £20 per day including lunch, and if you book for the two days, it's £35 including lunch on both days.
Interviewer:	Do you reckon that the training would be enough to set a person up in a new career within the theatre or whatever?
Claire:	I think it would certainly help you decide if you'd thought about doing it, whether or not it's for you, because they are professionals who are leading the course, but they are also trained teachers – so they know how to get the message across. So, whether you've had experience or not, it might just set your mind thinking and suggest some new avenues maybe.
Interviewer:	Are you looking for any particular age group?
Claire:	Well, what we are generally saying is that this course is directed at adults especially, but any youngsters who've been working in this sort of activity are very welcome to come along.
Interviewer:	Right. Have you had successful events like this before?
Claire:	We ran a training day last year, when the focus was on acting and it was very, very successful and because of that, we came up with the idea of running another course.
Interviewer:	So, for people listening to this who'd like to be involved in this year's training weekend, how do they apply?
Claire:	If you're interested, whether you've got any experience or not, do ring me. My name is Claire Ewington …
Interviewer:	I'll just make a note of this because if I write the listeners will have time to do so as well.
Claire:	… and that's spelt E-W-I-N-G-T-O-N and your best bet is to phone me directly at the theatre for more information or to book your place. And it's a city number, so that's 01773 578926.
Interviewer:	And you're the Education Manager at the theatre, aren't you?
Claire:	That's right and, of course, we have many other educational projects throughout the year.
Interviewer:	So, anyone interested in those could also call you.
Claire:	Indeed.
Interviewer:	Thank you very much, Claire, and all the best for the training weekend.
Claire:	Thank you.

[pause]

Now you'll hear Part Two again.

tone

[The recording is repeated.]

[pause]

That's the end of Part Two.

Now turn to Part Three.

[pause]

PART 3

You will hear five different students who are studying away from home. They are talking about their accommodation. For questions 19 to 23, choose from the list A to F what each speaker says about their accommodation. Use the letters only once. There is one extra letter which you do not need to use.

You now have thirty seconds in which to look at Part Three.

[Pause the recording here for 30 seconds.]

tone

Speaker 1

[pause]

I'd requested college accommodation, so when I was offered it I was really pleased. I didn't fancy having to look after myself … too many other things to do … lessons and homework and going out with friends. I knew what the rules were – in by ten, no noise after nine – and I didn't mind them at first, but they've started to annoy me more and more – and now I can't wait to get out and be able to do my own thing. I don't think I'll be recommending this place to anyone else!

[pause]

Speaker 2

[pause]

It's exciting leaving home and becoming independent. I've been staying with some relatives for the past year. I'd stayed with them before so when I knew I was coming here to study they said, why don't you come and live with us – great. And they've been fine – let me do whatever I want and haven't stuck to rigid meal times and all that sort of thing. So I've been able to meet plenty of people and get to know the area and the course and so on. I feel a part of it all now, but I'm always ready to try something different.

[pause]

Speaker 3

[pause]

I was pretty calm about coming here, but I couldn't decide whether to stay with a family or get my own flat. I'd talked to other people, you know, friends who've studied away from home before and they all recommended that I should get a flat because you have so much more freedom, so I did that. I'd only been here two weeks and I went out one day and left the front door unlocked. When I got back, I found that my camera had been stolen. I suppose I was lucky it was just that. I'm a bit more careful now.

[pause]

Speaker 4

[pause]

My friend Benny and I started the course at the same time. There was never any doubt that we'd share a place. It was the obvious choice for us to make and I think it's definitely the best option. Of course, you have to think about what you're going to eat, have some kind of system for cleaning, a few ground rules. We get annoyed with each other at times. Benny smokes and I had to ask him to go outside, which he does now. It hasn't all been straightforward but overall I prefer the independence this place gives me.

[pause]

Speaker 5

[pause]

My sister came here before me and studied at the same college. She told my parents that it would be much better if I stayed with her and then she could look after me, help me settle down here, that kind of thing. So, that's what happened – nobody asked me what I wanted to do. Well, the truth is we don't get on badly but I never seem to see the other students that I study with, which is a big disadvantage. I think it's better to force yourself to find your own way in a new environment.

[pause]

Now you'll hear Part Three again.

tone

[The recording is repeated.]

[pause]

That's the end of Part Three.

Now turn to Part Four.

[pause]

PART 4

You will hear part of a radio interview in which Tina White, a magazine editor, talks about her life and work. For questions 24 to 30, choose the best answer A, B or C.

You now have one minute in which to look at Part Four.

[Pause the recording here for one minute.]

tone

Interviewer: Tina White, some people describe you as the best magazine editor in the world, and you are only in your thirties. Can you tell us how you started your amazing career?

Tina: Well, when I was twenty, still at college, I was asked to write a weekly column for a local paper. The paper had wanted me to write about famous people, you know, their wonderful lifestyles, the sort of thing people like to read about. Instead, what I did was to concentrate on people who the general public didn't know, but who had something original to say.

Interviewer:	And you got away with it! Now at that early stage, your family was important. How far did they influence your career choice?
Tina:	My father was a film producer, and my childhood was spent around international actors and directors, so with such influences, I should have become an actress – something my father would have loved. But no, I chose to be a journalist in spite of the wishes of my family. I think the biggest influence was my school, not so much the people but the materials it gave me access to … the hours and hours spent in the library.
Interviewer:	From being a journalist, you then went on to become an editor. I understand the first magazine you edited, *Female Focus*, wasn't much of a success?
Tina:	Well, I was the editor for a year, and then I resigned, mainly because of disagreements with the owners. They were reluctant to change things, because they had faith it would eventually make a profit. But when you think of it, the magazine had been losing millions of pounds a year before I became its editor. When I left, it was still losing money but nothing like as much as previously. Also, when I took over, it was selling around 650,000 copies. That soon increased to 800,000, so it was certainly an improvement.
Interviewer:	And now you are editing *Woman's World*, and you've made it the best selling women's magazine ever. How do you make people want to read it?
Tina:	For some of my competitors, the most important point is what you put on the cover of your magazine. But they forget faithful readers look beyond that. The real challenge is, how do you encourage a reader to read a serious piece? How are we going to make it an article that people want to read? You have to get their attention. And nothing does that better than a very lively, even shocking, opening line.
Interviewer:	It is said that you work very hard because you don't trust your employees.
Tina:	That *was* the case five years ago, when I was appointed. It almost drove me mad. I knew I had the right idea, for example, but I wasn't able to get it done because I didn't have the brilliant writers I have now, or the right staff to read all the material when it came in. I had to read everything about six times, and that was awful! It took me four years to put together the team I wanted, and it would be very unfair to say I don't trust them.
Interviewer:	Do you sometimes worry that you might lose your fame and wealth?
Tina:	Yes, when you work as an editor, you are praised today and criticised tomorrow. Of course it would be difficult to live without all the … well … material comforts I'm used to, but a smaller income is something I think I could cope with. It wouldn't be the end of the world. Much more serious would be if the people I work with no longer admired my work, and most of all I want it to stay that way.
Interviewer:	And what about the future?
Tina:	Well, people often think I have planned my career very carefully, but in fact lots of things have happened by chance. Lots of opportunities have come my way, and I was once asked to edit a book series. As a youngster, one of my dreams was to be a writer, to write a novel that would become a best-seller and then an award-winning film. Well, it may seem silly, but I still hope that will happen one day.
Interviewer:	Tina, thank you very much for joining us today.

[pause]

Now you'll hear Part Four again.

tone

[The recording is repeated.]

[pause]

That's the end of Part Four.
There'll now be a pause of five minutes for you to copy your answers onto the separate answer sheet.

[pause]

[Teacher, pause the recording here for five minutes. Remind your students when they have one minute left.]

[pause]

That's the end of the test. Please stop now. Your supervisor will now collect all the question papers and answer sheets.

Goodbye.

Test 3 Key

Paper 1   Reading (1 hour 15 minutes)

Part 1

1 C   2 H   3 F   4 A   5 G   6 E   7 B

Part 2

8 C   9 A   10 A   11 B   12 D   13 C   14 A   15 B

Part 3

16 F   17 H   18 E   19 A   20 C   21 G   22 B

Part 4

23 C   24 D   25 A   26 B   27/28 C/D (*in either order*)
29 C   30 B   31 E   32 F   33 E   34/35 F/D (*in either order*)

Paper 2   Writing (1 hour 30 minutes)

Task-specific mark schemes

Part 1

Question 1

Content
Major points: Letter must include all the points in the notes.
1) recommend the earlier trip, as it is less crowded
2) explain why a guided tour is essential
3) suggest taking a picnic
4) suggest trying water sport(s)
5) give information about group booking

Organisation and cohesion
Letter format, with early reference to why the person is writing. Clear organisation of points. Suitable opening and closing formulae.

Appropriacy of register and format
Informal letter.

Range
Language appropriate for recommending, giving reasons, making a suggestion and giving information.

Target reader
Would have enough information to decide about the trip.

Part 2

Question 2

Content
Report should give suggestions about how often the club should meet, what type of activities it should organise and how the club could be advertised.

Range
Language of making suggestions and vocabulary appropriate to organising an English language club.

Organisation and cohesion
Report should be clearly organised. Sub-headings would be an advantage. There should be an introduction and a conclusion.

Appropriacy of register and format
Register could range from the neutral to the formal, but must be consistent throughout. Formal report layout is not essential.

Target reader
Would be informed about the writer's suggestions for the organisation of the club.

Question 3

Content
Story should continue from the prompt sentence.

Range
Past tenses. Vocabulary appropriate to chosen topic for story.

Organisation and cohesion
Could be minimally paragraphed. Story should reach a definite ending, even if that ending is somewhat open-ended, as in many modern short stories.

Appropriacy of register and format
Consistent neutral or informal narrative.

Target reader
Would be able to follow the storyline.

Question 4

Content
Article should describe the difference it would make in the writer's life to have to live without television for a week.

Range
Language of description and comparison.

Organisation and cohesion
Clear development of description with appropriate linking and paragraphing.

Appropriacy of register and format
Register could range from informal to neutral, but must be consistent throughout.

Target reader
Would be informed about the difference the lack of television would make to the writer.

Question 5(a)

Content
Writer should say whether anything in the book or short story disappointed him/her.

Range
Language of description and narration.

Organisation and cohesion
Clear organisation of composition with appropriate paragraphing.

Appropriacy of register and format
Neutral composition.

Target reader
Would be informed about whether the candidate was disappointed or not with reference to the book or short story read.

Question 5(b)

Content
Clear reference to characters from the book or short story and the importance of the relationships between them.

Range
Language of description, narration and explanation of views.

Organisation and cohesion
Clear development of description and narration leading up to explaining the candidate's viewpoint, with appropriate linking and paragraphing.

Appropriacy of register and format
Neutral composition.

Target reader
Would be informed about the importance of the relationships between characters.

Paper 3 Use of English (1 hour 15 minutes)

Part 1

1 C	2 B	3 B	4 C	5 D	6 B	7 C	8 C	9 A
10 D	11 A	12 C	13 D	14 C	15 B			

Part 2

16 did/tried	17 with/over	18 such	19 to	20 those
21 only/just	22 could/would	23 in	24 as	25 were
26 it	27 nothing	28 but/although	29 which	30 for

Part 3

31 be produced | **by** this company
32 to talk | to him **again**
33 **my** holiday | I had

34 **ought** to | have locked
35 any **chance** | of Pete
36 from Paul | **nobody** has
37 got | **used** to
38 **felt** like | doing
39 being **unable** | to sing
40 as **soon** as | we arrive

Part 4

41 place   42 being   43 in   44 have   45 by   46 ✓
47 which   48 had   49 either   50 there   51 it   52 of
53 having   54 too   55 ✓

Part 5

56 attractive   57 tourists   58 achievement   59 employee
60 originality   61 communication(s)   62 unclear   63 traditional
64 success   65 appearance

Paper 4   Listening (40 minutes approximately)

Part 1

1 C   2 B   3 A   4 B   5 B   6 A   7 C   8 B

Part 2

9 south of France   10 1970   11 famous people   12 (young) children
13 (about) 50%   14 under (the) water   15 breathe (out)   16 (try to) float
17 (feeling) confident   18 3 hours/lessons

Part 3

19 C   20 B   21 D   22 F   23 E

Part 4

24 F   25 T   26 F   27 F   28 F   29 T   30 T

Transcript   *First Certificate Listening Test. Test Three.*
Hello. I'm going to give you the instructions for this test. I'll introduce
each part of the test and give you time to look at the questions. At the start
of each piece you'll hear this sound:

tone

You'll hear each piece twice.

Remember, while you're listening, write your answers on the question
paper. You'll have time at the end of the test to copy your answers onto
the separate answer sheet.

There will now be a pause. Please ask any questions now, because you must not speak during the test.

[pause]

PART 1

Now open your question paper and look at Part One.

[pause]

You'll hear people talking in eight different situations. For questions 1 to 8, choose the best answer, A, B or C.

Question 1

One.
You overhear a man talking about an experience he had at an airport. What did he lose?
A   his passport
B   his wallet
C   a piece of luggage

[pause]

tone

Man: The airport staff looked everwhere for it. It was terrible. I thought the plane was going to go without me. At first I thought someone must have taken it. Although my money wasn't inside, I'd bought some nice presents for the family. Then I remembered that I'd been to the washroom and I must have put it down in there. Luckily, I had my documents and boarding card in my jacket pocket and, to cut a long story short, I had to get on the plane without it. The airport staff sent it on to me three days later.

[pause]

tone

[The recording is repeated.]

[pause]

Question 2

Two.
You hear an advertisement on the radio.
What is special about the Fretlight guitar?
A   It plays recorded music.
B   It teaches you how to play.
C   It plugs into a computer.

[pause]

tone

Man: The *Fretlight* is a fully functional guitar that comes in acoustic and electric models. Built into its body is an on-board computer and 132 lights that show you where to put your fingers. Simply flip a switch and choose the chord or note that you would like to play, and the finger positions for making the appropriate notes will be promptly displayed on the neck of the guitar. Beginners can get a real feel for the fingerboard, while the more experienced players will be able to discover lots of new musical possibilities …

[pause]

tone

[The recording is repeated.]

[pause]

Question 3   *Three.*
You hear part of a radio programme.
What is the presenter talking about?
A   food safety
B   meal times
C   healthy recipes

[pause]

tone

Presenter: Whether you have just one large meal a day, or a number of small meals, there are some basic steps to keep you in good health. Ideally, eat food as soon as it is cooked or prepared. If you are preparing food for later use, keep cold foods in the fridge and hot foods hot until they are ready to be eaten. Piping hot, that's how cooked food should be, especially when it's reheated. And remember, prepared foods left at room temperature will not keep long, however fresh the ingredients you have used.

[pause]

tone

[The recording is repeated.]

[pause]

Question 4   *Four.*
You hear two people discussing a type of pollution.
What do the speakers agree about?
A   the best way to solve the problem
B   how they feel about this type of pollution
C   how they reacted to the solution they saw

[pause]

tone

Woman: Do you know what they were doing in town the other day? I had to rush away because it set my teeth on edge, but they were chipping the chewing gum off the paths with sharp tools.
Man: You know, I only realised recently that all those black spots on the ground are actually old chewing gum.
Woman: I mean, it's disgusting, isn't it?
Man: Deeply.

| Woman: | And what a nasty job! |
| Man: | Well, I was actually there when the city once tested out a machine for this and, I had to laugh, it needed such a powerful suck to get it off, it lifted the stones themselves. |

[pause]

tone

[The recording is repeated.]

[pause]

Question 5

Five.
You hear a conversation between a shop assistant and a customer about a compact disc.
What was the cause of the problem?
A   The customer gave the wrong number.
B   A mistake was made on the order form.
C   The disc was incorrectly labelled.

[pause]

tone

Shop asst:	And you ordered it two weeks ago? Well, I can't find anything in the order book … Oh, yes, here it is. Well, it seems we chased it up after you phoned and they said they couldn't find the order, so we gave them the details again. It hasn't turned up though. Oh, perhaps … here's a note on the order form. They then told us there's nothing under the number you gave us, I'm afraid.
Customer:	Well, I noted it down very carefully. Look.
Shop asst:	Uh-huh. Oh, I see. Two figures are the wrong way round on our form, that's why they couldn't find the disc.

[pause]

tone

[The recording is repeated.]

[pause]

Question 6

Six.
You overhear a conversation at a football game.
What does the speaker say about his team?
A   They're better than usual.
B   They're as good as he expected.
C   They tend to be unlucky.

[pause]

tone

| Man 1: | Not many here today, are there? |

Man 2: I guess it isn't as popular as it used to be. A few years ago it was so crowded here, you were lucky if you could see over all the heads. This is the first time I've been this season. I was expecting to see them lose – as ever – but I can't wait for the second half if they carry on playing like this.

[pause]

tone

[The recording is repeated.]

[pause]

Question 7 | *Seven.*
You overhear a schoolgirl talking to her friend.
What does she think about her new teacher?
A He is clever.
B He is funny.
C He is interesting.

[pause]

tone

Girl: It's funny, I've had loads of maths teachers and they all seemed to be the same – really clever with figures but useless at dealing with children. That's why I used to play about in lessons and do anything for a laugh. But Mr Jones is something else. He's quite serious and he makes us work really hard and gives us loads of problems to solve, but what I like is he relates everything to real life.

[pause]

tone

[The recording is repeated.]

[pause]

Question 8 | *Eight.*
In a hotel you overhear a conversation.
Who is the woman?
A a tour guide
B a tourist
C a hotel receptionist

[pause]

tone

Man: Oh, by the way, what's this all-island trip like then?
Woman: It lasts all day and you get picked up from the hotel at about 7.30 and they take you around the island to look at the sights.
Man: Do you think it's worth going on then?
Woman: I'd say so. You see all the sights and have lunch in a restaurant by the sea. The price includes everything, you know, like the museum and everything. The whole family enjoyed it when we went.

[pause]

tone

[The recording is repeated.]

[pause]

That's the end of Part One.

Now turn to Part Two.

[pause]

PART 2   *You will hear part of a radio interview with a swimming instructor. For questions 9 to 18, complete the sentences.*

You now have forty-five seconds in which to look at Part Two.

[Pause the recording here for 45 seconds.]

tone

Interviewer:	And now for our sports section, and I have with me today Paul Collison who is a swimming instructor with a rather unusual approach. Thanks for taking the time during your holiday to come and talk to us, Paul.
Paul:	It's very kind of you to invite me.
Interviewer:	Paul – you're *the* swimming instructor at the Palace Hotel in the south of France. How long have you been there?
Paul:	Oh, well I started working there in 1970 when I was 18 years old.
Interviewer:	And you've never moved?
Paul:	Nope – I get to meet a lot of famous people there and … I guess I enjoy that.
Interviewer:	And of course a lot of them go there because they want *you* to teach them to swim!
Paul:	That's true, but I teach plenty of other people too – and not all my students are beginners.
Interviewer:	But we're not talking about young children, are we?
Paul:	Not usually – there isn't the same challenge teaching children. They have an almost natural ability to swim. Adults are afraid, and helping them overcome that is hard but much more fun somehow.
Interviewer:	But don't a lot of people just give up trying to learn once they reach a certain age?
Paul:	Not at all. I get hundreds of calls from people looking for 'sympathetic' instructors. I would estimate that about 50% of the adult population can't swim – but they're still keen to learn.
Interviewer:	So it's just fear that holds them back?
Paul:	Basically, yes. I come across it all the time and it isn't just beginners. I have students who can swim a bit, but don't make any progress because – like all of them – they hate going *under* water.
Interviewer:	Mmm … So what's the secret, Paul?
Paul:	Well, you've got to relax in the water and that means that you *must* control your breathing.
Interviewer:	And I understand you have a special technique to help people do that.
Paul:	Yes, before my students even go into the pool I teach them how to breathe and to do that I give everyone a salad bowl.
Interviewer:	A salad bowl? Right …

Paul:	Everyone in the group gets one of these … each full of water. First, I get them to breathe … slowly through the nose and mouth … just normal controlled breathing.
Interviewer:	To calm them.
Paul:	Uhuh … and then – they all have to put their faces in the bowl and breathe out under water.
Interviewer:	How does it go?
Paul:	Well, they're all terrified at first. So we repeat the exercise many times and in the end they become quite competitive about who can keep their face down the longest!
Interviewer:	And that means they've started to forget about their fear.
Paul:	Exactly. When I'm sure they're more confident about breathing, I move the group into the pool and I tell them that they are going to begin by trying to float with their faces in the water. Once I'm sure they're OK, I start them off and I teach different swimming strokes to different pupils depending on which one I think they'll find easiest. The swimming technique itself is far less important than feeling confident in the water.
Interviewer:	Great. So how many lessons would I need to learn to swim?
Paul:	Well, all my lessons are an hour long and generally it just takes three to overcome the fear and get people swimming. A few never make it but I'd say 90% end up swimmers.
Interviewer:	So there's hope for us all yet … and now on to …

[pause]

Now you'll hear Part Two again.

tone

[The recording is repeated.]

[pause]

That's the end of Part Two.

Now turn to Part Three.

[pause]

PART 3

You'll hear part of a radio programme called 'Morning Market'. Five listeners have telephoned the programme because they have something to sell. For questions 19 to 23, choose which of the statements A to F matches the reason each of the people gives for selling their possession. Use the letters only once. There's one extra letter which you do not need to use.

You now have thirty seconds in which to look at Part Three.

[Pause the recording here for 30 seconds.]

tone

Speaker 1

[pause]

I've got a brand-new rowing machine. I won it actually, about two months ago, and it's still in its box. It's got an electric timer on it which tells you how much rowing you've done and all that. So anyone who's into exercise can do lots of rowing and keep fit and healthy. It folds up really small, so, you know, it won't take up too much space in, like, a bedroom or anything. I mean, I'll never use it because I was after the holiday which was won by whoever came first in the competition. So I'm looking for around forty-five pounds and my number is …

[pause]

Speaker 2

[pause]

I've got a kidney-shaped bath, colour soft cream, for sale. It's still in its original packing case because I ordered the wrong colour, you know, it didn't go with the rest of the bathroom suite I'd got. So, I contacted, you know, the suppliers who said they'll send me a replacement, at a price, of course! But I've now got to get rid of this one. It cost originally a hundred and seventy-five pounds and I'm letting it go for fifty if anyone's interested. OK? My number's …

[pause]

Speaker 3

[pause]

I've got a real bargain. It's a Lieberstein electric organ and it's got two keyboards and a rhythm section. It's in good condition, plays quite well, and it's not difficult to use or anything. But, what with us having a baby on the way, it's got to make way for more essential items, as we've only got a tiny flat at the moment. So, as I say, if anyone wants it, they can make me an offer. The only problem is anyone interested would have to come and collect it. The number to ring is …

[pause]

Speaker 4

[pause]

Hallo. I've got a ladies' cycle for sale. I've got back trouble and I've been advised not to ride it, so rather than be tempted, I'll get rid of it. I hate the idea, because we're not well-served with public transport out here and I used it quite a lot, but as I daren't ride it any more, I think it would be a mistake to hang on to it, you know, in case I had second thoughts. So, it's a Raleigh Chopper, pink, and I'd like thirty-five pounds for it, please. I can be contacted on …

[pause]

Speaker 5

[pause]

I've got two frying pans, you know, the sort for cooking stir-fry in, and a seven-piece tool set to go with them. All boxed and everything. Anyway, they've hardly been used because at one time I was intending to do a lot of this type of cooking because I've only got a small kitchenette, like, no oven. But I've been given a microwave instead now, so much easier to use. So, that's ten pounds for both pans and the tools and my number is …

[pause]

Now you'll hear Part Three again.

tone

[The recording is repeated.]

[pause]

That's the end of Part Three.

Now turn to Part Four.

[pause]

PART 4   *You'll hear a radio interview with Peter Manson about the job he does for a record company. For questions 24 to 30, decide which of the statements are TRUE and which are FALSE. Write T for TRUE or F for FALSE.*

You now have forty-five seconds in which to look at Part Four.

[Pause the recording here for 45 seconds.]

tone

Interviewer: So, Peter, as far as I understand it, with record companies in Britain fiercely competing to find good new bands, your job is to look for talented young musicians?

Peter Manson: That's right. In the 1980s, record companies stopped actively looking for new talent because they were reissuing old hits on compact disc, but now that is no longer profitable.

Interviewer: So now they are employing people like you?

Peter Manson: Yes, when we find a good artist or band, we sign them up, that is we sign a contract with them. There's a flood of small bands and other new artists. I recently signed up an 18-year-old schoolboy who had produced two excellent recordings from his bedroom! My job is not an easy one because surprisingly most young artists are really quiet people, not at all out-going and they try to avoid publicity.

Interviewer: How do you find your new bands?

Peter Manson: Well, it's a bit of a lottery. One will turn up when you're not even looking for it. That's what makes life interesting for me. I'll give you an example. In the summer of 1993, I happened to be in a record shop in Oxford, and I met a guy that played bass for a local band called 'Loops'. A few days later I went to see them play in a tent on Oxford Park, as part of an extremely wet music festival. The band proved to be superb.

Interviewer: So you signed them up for your company?

Peter Manson: Well, they had begun to be followed around by other 'talent spotters' like myself. It took me three months from when I first saw them, before I could persuade them to sign a contract. They liked me, but the main reason was I had seen them first. That sort of thing makes it all worthwhile.

Interviewer: So do things ever get nasty?

Peter Manson:	Well, I'm not perfect, but some people in the music business will do dishonest things. One of my competitors once went as far as sending expensive presents to a band he and I wanted to sign up.
Interviewer:	Do you rely on contacts for information?
Peter Manson:	Oh, certainly. Lots of contracts will result from information I get from contacts. But you must make sure they are good sources. Once I found myself in a threatening situation, when two big, strong men brought a tape into my office and demanded I listen to it. For six months after that I received frightening threats.
Interviewer:	So your life is not as glamorous as it seems …
Peter Manson:	Well, in my profession, we spend a lot of time at musical venues, but in fact we can't just relax and enjoy ourselves. You find yourself going to more and more shows, hoping to spot someone a bit special. You often don't even see the whole show as you can quickly spot those with talent and those without.
Interviewer:	It must be exhausting!
Peter Manson:	Yes, we live in fear of not attending the obscure show that might have led to the big, important contract, missing the little band who might just turn out to be the next week's heroes. Sometimes you miss things simply by not being early enough. And of course all the time we must also look after the bands we already have contracts with.
Interviewer:	Well, you seem to be doing extremely well, anyway.
Peter Manson:	Oh, yes! My greatest moment was only a couple of months ago. This band, having only played together a couple of times, drove to this venue and demanded to be allowed to play a song. I was in the audience, they started to play, and after hearing just a few notes on the guitar, shouted that I'd just discovered the future of rock 'n' roll and jumped on the stage to sign them! Fortunately it turned out later that they could sing as well!
Interviewer:	The story must bring tears to your rivals' eyes. Well, we certainly wish you the best of luck with this new band! Peter Manson, thank you very much for talking to us.

[pause]

Now you'll hear Part Four again.

tone

[The recording is repeated.]

[pause]

That's the end of Part Four.
There'll now be a pause of five minutes for you to copy your answers onto the separate answer sheet.

[Teacher, pause the recording here for five minutes.
Remind your students when they have one minute left.]

That's the end of the test. Please stop now. Your supervisor will now collect all the question papers and answer sheets. Goodbye.

Test 4 Key

Paper 1 Reading (1 hour 15 minutes)

Part 1

1 C   2 A   3 G   4 B   5 F   6 H   7 E

Part 2

8 B   9 C   10 A   11 D   12 A   13 B   14 C   15 C

Part 3

16 B   17 C   18 E   19 H   20 D   21 F   22 A

Part 4

23 C   24 D   25 B   26 A   27 E   28 A   29 C
30 A   31 D   32 C   33 B   34 E   35 D

Paper 2 Writing (1 hour 30 minutes)

Task-specific mark schemes

Part 1

Question 1

Content

Major points: The letter must:
1) be positive about the good programme arranged by Mr Robertson
2) point out at least one thing especially appreciated
3) explain that all the students would like to go to the London Fashion and Leisure Show
4) give at least one reason why they want to go
5) suggest how the programme could be changed.

N.B. Coverage of the first point may not explicitly include 'thanks'. The 'thanks' may be implicit.

Organisation and cohesion
Letter format, with early reference to why the person is writing. Clear organisation of points with suitable paragraphing. Suitable opening and closing formulae.

Appropriacy of register and format
Formal letter.

Range
Language appropriate for explaining, making a request and making a suggestion.

Target reader
Would have enough information to act on and respond to the writer's letter.

Part 2

Question 2

Content
Composition could agree or disagree with the proposition, or discuss both sides of the argument.

Range
Language of opinion and explanation. Vocabulary relevant to the way the topic is explored.

Organisation and cohesion
Clear development of viewpoint with appropriate paragraphing and linking of ideas.

Appropriacy of register and format
Neutral composition.

Target reader
Would be able to understand the writer's viewpoint.

Question 3

Content
Article should state ways in which people's homes in the future will be different and/or ways in which they might be the same. (Acceptable to say or imply that nothing will be the same.)

Range
Language of description. Possibly explanation. Vocabulary relating to homes / the future.

Organisation and cohesion
Clear development of ideas, with appropriate linking and paragraphing.

Appropriacy of register and format
Register could range from the informal to the formal, but must be consistent throughout.

Target reader
Would be clearly informed.

Question 4

Content
Story should continue from the prompt sentence in the first person.

Range
Past tenses. Vocabulary appropriate to the chosen topic for the story.

Organisation and cohesion
Could be minimally paragraphed. Should reach a definite ending.

Appropriacy of register and format
Consistently neutral or informal narrative.

Target reader
Would be able to follow the storyline.

Question 5(a)

Content
Writer can agree or disagree with the statement, and explain why with reference to the book or story read.

Range
Language of opinion and explanation.

Organisation and cohesion
Clear development of viewpoint with appropriate paragraphing and linking of ideas.

Appropriacy of register and format
Neutral composition.

Target reader
Would be able to understand the writer's point of view.

Question 5(b)

Content
Writer should inform their pen friend whether the book or short story read would be a suitable present for the pen friend's cousin's fifteenth birthday.

Range
Language of opinion, explanation and possibly recommendation.

Organisation and cohesion
Clear development of viewpoint with appropriate paragraphing and linking of ideas.

Appropriacy of register and format
Informal letter.

Target reader
Would be informed as to whether to give the book or short story as a present to the fifteen-year-old.

Paper 3 Use of English (1 hour 15 minutes)

Part 1

| 1 D | 2 C | 3 D | 4 B | 5 D | 6 C | 7 B | 8 C |
| 9 C | 10 D | 11 A | 12 B | 13 C | 14 D | 15 D | |

Part 2

16 take   **17** not   **18** been   **19** need/have   **20** of/with/in
21 each   **22** far   **23** While/As/When   **24** are/get   **25** on
26 the/these   **27** get/climb   **28** in   **29** which   **30** first/times

Part 3

31 **took** my car | didn't
32 never seen | such a **strange**
33 were **driven** | into town by
34 **insisted** on | paying
35 didn't **succeed** | in persuading
36 you **mind** | not using
37 not seen Mark **since** | last
38 made a **good** | impression on
39 **wishes** (that) he had | told
40 had **trouble** | (in) following

Part 4

41 who   **42** ✓   **43** ✓   **44** for   **45** all   **46** ✓
47 just   **48** ✓   **49** out   **50** they   **51** much   **52** any
53 by   **54** been   **55** ✓

Part 5

56 extraordinary   **57** freezing/frozen   **58** assistance   **59** equipment
60 loneliness   **61** hopeful   **62** friendships   **63** heat
64 poisonous   **65** reasonable

Paper 4   Listening (40 minutes approximately)

Part 1

1 A   **2** A   **3** B   **4** A   **5** C   **6** A   **7** C   **8** C

Part 2

9 circle (around them)   **10** (a) brain(s)   **11** stress
12 feelings   **13** read   **14** reward   **15** 52 teeth   **16** two days
17 sound wave(s)/sound(s) / high-pitched noises   **18** (fishing) nets

Part 3

19 E   **20** F   **21** C   **22** D   **23** B

Part 4

24 A   **25** C   **26** B   **27** A   **28** A   **29** C   **30** B

Transcript
First Certificate Listening Test. Test Four.
Hello. I'm going to give you the instructions for this test. I'll introduce each part of the test and give you time to look at the questions. At the start of each piece you'll hear this sound:

tone

You'll hear each piece twice.

Remember, while you're listening, write your answers on the question paper. You'll have time at the end of the test to copy your answers onto the separate answer sheet.

There will now be a pause. Please ask any questions now, because you must not speak during the test.

[pause]

Now open your question paper and look at Part One.

[pause]

PART 1
You'll hear people talking in eight different situations. For questions 1 to 8, choose the best answer, A, B or C.

Question 1
One.
You overhear some people talking at a party in a hotel. Where did the people first meet each other?
A   at school
B   at work
C   at a wedding

[pause]

tone

Man:	Is Mark Hobson here?
Woman:	He's got a crisis at work and couldn't come. But Julie's here somewhere. Did you know he married Julie? You know, the girl who could never spell anything!
Man:	Oh, right.
Woman:	It's their wedding anniversary today, actually. She says she'd rather be here with her childhood friends than waiting at home for Mark to finish work!
Man:	Has he changed much?
Woman:	Well, he looks much the same as he did all those years ago.

[pause]

tone

[The recording is repeated.]

[pause]

Question 2	*Two.*
	You overhear a conversation in a restaurant.
	Why haven't they seen each other lately?
	A He has been too busy.
	B He has been ill.
	C He has been away.

[pause]

tone

Man:	Hello, Jean!
Woman:	Mike Carstairs! My favourite customer. You haven't been in for ages.
Man:	No, I haven't, that's right.
Woman:	How are you?
Man:	I'm fine. I heard you weren't well.
Woman:	Well, I was away for a couple of weeks. But I'm fine now. Ah! You were going to the States, weren't you?
Man:	That fell through.
Woman:	Oh, did it?
Man:	What I've been doing is reorganising the whole department non-stop since I saw you. Just haven't had a moment to myself. This is the first time I've been in here since Christmas.
Woman:	Well, it's good to see you. Are you ready to order?

[pause]

tone

[The recording is repeated.]

[pause]

Question 3	*Three.*
	You overhear someone talking about a concert.
	How did she feel at the time?
	A angry
	B frightened
	C disappointed

[pause]

tone

Girl:	It was really awful and I'd been so looking forward to it. Don't get me wrong – the music was brilliant and the show itself was really well done, but I'm sure they let too many people in – it was ever so crowded. I was right at the front and everyone was pushing me against the stage. I couldn't breathe and I was so scared I thought I was going to faint.

[pause]

tone

[The recording is repeated.]

[pause]

Question 4	*Four.* *You hear a writer of children's stories talking about books and compact discs.* *What advantage does he think books have over compact discs?* A *They may last for a longer time.* B *They are easier to look after.* C *They contain better quality material.*

[pause]

tone

Man: I was brought up with a respect for books, you know, always having clean hands, not bending the pages down, etc. and I certainly try to make sure mine are as well-made as possible. I like to pick them up by the wrong bit and throw them around and so on, you know, to make sure they are strong. I think it's the permanence of books that sets them apart from the other media, don't you? Of course, what's more important is that you have good literature and good images and, I suppose, whether that's actually on a compact disc or in a book doesn't matter.

[pause]

tone

[The recording is repeated.]

[pause]

Question 5	*Five.* *You hear a husband and wife talking about their summer holidays.* *What problem do they have?* A *They really hate flying anywhere.* B *They can never think of anywhere to go.* C *They never agree about what to do.*

[pause]

tone

Husband: You see right from the time we first met it was obvious that Natalie and I wanted a particular kind of holiday – the trouble was, it wasn't the same! I like going off and doing my own thing. You know, history and museums – that's what interests me.

Wife: Well, I love markets and looking for bargains – so we end up sort of hating each other for two weeks or so, instead of having a really nice time together. The odd thing is that we see eye to eye all the rest of the time. It's just when we step on that plane – then the trouble starts!

[pause]

tone

[The recording is repeated.]

[pause]

Question 6   Six.
You hear a researcher being asked about her work.
What is she doing when she speaks?
A   denying an accusation
B   disproving a theory
C   accepting a criticism

[pause]

tone

Interviewer: Now it's a bit suspicious that this research about glasses has been paid for by a contact lens company, isn't it? Is it genuine or are you having us on?
Researcher: Not at all. We asked about a thousand people, most of whom wore glasses, some of whom didn't, and really asked them what they thought of glasses. Their responses were interesting, but didn't come from us; it's what they told us answering open-ended questions. And most of them said, while they thought that glasses could be, you know, pretty trendy and that some of them looked quite cool, that they didn't much like them.

[pause]

tone

[The recording is repeated.]

[pause]

Question 7   Seven.
You overhear a woman talking to a friend on a train.
What does the woman think of the course she has attended?
A   It has made her feel more confident.
B   It has made her feel less confident.
C   It hasn't made much difference to how she feels.

[pause]

tone

Woman: Well, the whole point was to build confidence and I'm sure most feel it succeeded, even if only partly. I must say I found it all very enjoyable, although I can't say I've benefited greatly. There was plenty of opportunity to get to know other people in the business, though, if you wanted to – you know the sort of thing, trips to restaurants and the theatre in the evenings.

[pause]

tone

[The recording is repeated.]

[pause]

Question 8	Eight. *You overhear a woman speaking on the radio.* *What is she doing?* A complaining about something B apologising for something C explaining something

[pause]

tone

Man:	So, shall we move on to the next subject?
Woman:	I'm sorry, but I do think it's necessary to go through this again for the benefit of your listeners. Look, this is a crucial point and I don't think it can be stressed enough. As I was saying, the first thing that anyone with a complaint about their pension should do is put it in writing.

[pause]

tone

[The recording is repeated.]

[pause]

That's the end of Part One.

Now turn to Part Two.

[pause]

PART 2	*You'll hear a radio report about dolphins. For questions 9 to 18, complete the sentences.* *You now have forty-five seconds in which to look at Part Two.* [Pause the recording here for 45 seconds.] tone
Newsreader:	And for our last news item today, a special report from Diane Hassan on an animal that is rapidly becoming known as 'man's best friend', the dolphin.
Diane:	Last week, a 28-year-old diver who went swimming in the Red Sea with a group of dolphins, learnt the hard way just how caring these creatures can be. When the diver was suddenly attacked by a shark, they saved him by forming a circle around him and frightening the shark away. It's not the first time such a rescue has happened and it's been known for some time that dolphins will do for humans what they do for their own kind. They are, in fact, the only animals in the world whose brains match ours in terms of size, and their intelligence and ability to feel emotion continue to fascinate scientists and doctors alike. For some time now, their healing powers have been well known. A swim with a group of dolphins, for example, is a recognised 'medical' activity for everyday problems such as stress. But some dolphins are playing a far more serious medical role for us than that. Amanda Morton, who suffered from a life-threatening illness, argued that being with dolphins *saved her life* because they were able to read her feelings. 'They knew how I was feeling,'

she was quoted as saying. And it's the idea that they actually 'care', that they are gentle, happy creatures that want to befriend us, which has led to projects with children as well. In one such project, dolphins are being used to help children who are slow learners learn to read. The dolphins do things like carrying small boards on their noses. These boards show words or pictures which the children are asked to identify. When the children get it right, they spend more time swimming with the dolphins and touching them and they see this as a reward. So what is it that makes contact with dolphins so powerful? They certainly have an engaging smile … in each jaw they have up to 52 teeth, but rather than frightening us to death, it's one of the warmest greetings in the world! They're also fantastic swimmers to watch … the spotted dolphin has been observed reaching 20 miles an hour and keeping this up for two days at a time. And they *know* they're good at it so they show off in front of humans by diving in and out of the water and showing us just how much fun they're having. They're great communicators too. They make all kinds of fascinating high-pitched noises. They catch fish, for example, by sending out sound waves which tell them everything they need to know – where it is, what it is and how big it is.

The only creatures that concern dolphins, in fact, are sharks and *man*. We don't necessarily harm them on purpose, but we trap them in fishing nets and we pollute the water they swim in. Pollution, in fact, is one of the dolphin's greatest problems. So with all the good they do for us, isn't it time we started caring about them?

[pause]

Now you'll hear Part Two again.

tone

[The recording is repeated.]

[pause]

That's the end of Part Two.

Now turn to Part Three.

[pause]

PART 3

You'll hear five different people talking about the head teacher or principal of their former secondary school. For questions 19 to 23, choose from the list A to F what each speaker is saying. Use the letters only once. There's one extra letter which you do not need to use.

You now have thirty seconds in which to look at Part Three.

[Pause the recording here for 30 seconds.]

tone

Speaker 1

[pause]

It's strange looking back because at the time you don't always appreciate people and certainly I think that's true of your teachers and particularly a head teacher. I mean she was always encouraging us not to drop litter and to think about things like preserving the countryside and so on, and she'd say 'Don't you want your children to live in a better world?' But when you're fifteen, you can't imagine having a family – all you care about is getting your homework done and going out with your friends!

[pause]

Speaker 2

[pause]

I don't know if it's the same in all countries, but where I live your head teacher usually teaches classes too and we had our head for athletics. In one way it was exciting 'cos she was very good at it herself, like she could out-run any of the boys in our class, but whatever we were doing she was always pushing us to do it faster than anyone else or jump higher than our friends regardless of the talent or ability we had – and with some it was pointless.

[pause]

Speaker 3

[pause]

I think if it hadn't been for our head teacher, I'd be doing something quite different now. She used to assess our Art exams and although there were people in my class who were really talented artists … you know they could paint anything from real life and it looked brilliant … she always preferred the more unusual stuff – she said it showed we had ideas of our own, and she really liked that, so, I did well. I mean now I make a living putting designs on greeting cards.

[pause]

Speaker 4

[pause]

I always felt that our head teacher was under-valued and that she might have done better in a different environment … her own staff held her up a bit. They all seemed … oh, I don't know … maybe they just didn't like the idea of change … but I remember she wanted to introduce a new teaching method for French classes and the department head just dismissed the idea … and so many ideas she had which were never taken up are being used in schools today. I sometimes wonder how she feels.

[pause]

Speaker 5

[pause]

I've got some friends who say they left school and they suddenly felt lost. They'd spent a long time 'getting an education' but didn't know what to do once they'd got it. I think we were lucky because our head teacher built up a good network of contacts with local people and so they didn't mind giving us an insight into what it might be like, say, working in a hospital or office. I know it wasn't a new idea or anything but I think she gave us a good sense of direction which I've valued all my life.

[pause]

Now you'll hear Part Three again.

tone

[The recording is repeated.]

[pause]

That's the end of Part Three.

Now turn to Part Four.

[pause]

PART 4 | *You will hear an interview with a tour leader who works for an adventure company in Africa. For questions 24 to 30, choose the best answer A, B or C.*

You now have one minute in which to look at Part Four.

[Pause the recording here for one minute.]

Announcer:	And now for the holiday programme with Mandy Rice.
Mandy:	Today I'm talking to Don Nicholson, a tour leader who spends 10 months of the year looking after groups of up to 18 tourists in southern Africa. They travel together in the back of a truck, put up their own tents and cook their own food. Welcome to the programme, Don.
Don:	Thanks.
Mandy:	This is a holiday with a difference, isn't it? Tell us, first of all, what sort of people go on a camping trip in Africa … and a long one at that … it is a month each trip?
Don:	Yes. Well it sounds a sort of studenty thing to do, but in fact the majority of our passengers are people like doctors and lawyers. We do get some students but they tend to be the ones that are studying something like conservation or wildlife.
Mandy:	And when do they all first meet?
Don:	The evening before we set off. They fly in and I pick them up from the airport and immediately before we start sorting out places in the truck we go through what they've brought with them. Amazingly, every now and then we get somebody who genuinely doesn't realise it's a camping tour, so I have to rush out and get them blankets and a sleeping bag.
Mandy:	It must be difficult – a whole group of strangers coming together and then having to live together like that.
Don:	Mmm. It goes surprisingly well, but I always think the first day is critical because it sets the tone for the whole trip. We've had the odd nightmare start where we've got a flat tyre 20 minutes after we set off or it's dark and pouring with rain and people just can't get their tents up. Yeah, once we were making pasta late at night and the cook put in a tin of strawberry jam instead of tomato paste – those are the bad starts!
Mandy:	Basically everyone has to take part in the domestic chores, do they?
Don:	Yes. The brochure makes it clear that people have to work on a rota system and they usually do about an hour's work a day. We get a few who don't want to

muck in but more often they are just untidy and I've got a bit of an eye for that because … well, they might leave a fork lying on the ground, for example, and okay, it's just a fork, but in a lot of places in Africa you can't get forks, so I'm quite possessive about the equipment.

Mandy: And do people really get on?

Don: A lot of people have never lived in a tight community situation like this before and you do get conflicts and personality clashes. The best approach is to observe it from afar. If it gets out of hand, I might point out in front of the whole group that there's a problem between certain people.

Mandy: Shame them a bit … .

Don: Mmm. Sometimes it works. To be fair, conflicts are rare but small problems *can* mount up in that kind of environment. Evening noise, for example. Some people want to go to sleep early and others don't. On occasions I've had to be the sort of go-between and impose a 'lights out' time if things start getting out of hand.

Mandy: What about getting up, because that's something we're really not keen on on holiday?

Don: If we're going into a wildlife park we might have to be on the road by six a.m. but people still ask why they have to get up so early. I've learnt how to do it now. If they're a quick group I'll get them up at five, but if they're slow I won't shout and scream at them – I just get them up at four thirty.

Mandy: Well, perhaps now we should go on to talk about what there is to see in some of those game parks that you have to get up so early for.

[pause]

Now you'll hear Part Four again.

tone

[The recording is repeated.]

[pause]

That's the end of Part Four.
There'll now be a pause of five minutes for you to copy your answers onto the separate answer sheet.

[Teacher, pause the recording here for five minutes. Remind your students when they have one minute left.]

That's the end of the test. Please stop now. Your supervisor will now collect all the question papers and answer sheets.
Goodbye.

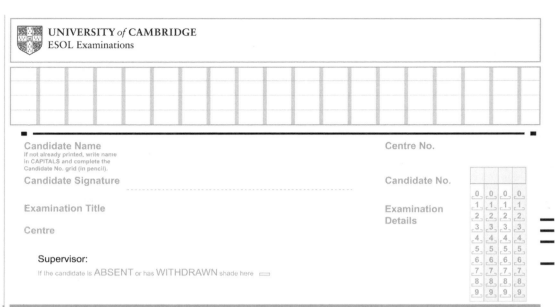

Candidate Answer Sheet: FCE Paper 1 Reading

Use a pencil

Mark ONE letter for each question.

For example, if you think B is the right answer to the question, mark your answer sheet like this:

0 | A B̶ C D E F G H I

Rub out any answer you wish to change with an eraser.

1 | A B C D E F G H I
2 | A B C D E F G H I
3 | A B C D E F G H I
4 | A B C D E F G H I
5 | A B C D E F G H I

6 | A B C D E F G H I
7 | A B C D E F G H I
8 | A B C D E F G H I
9 | A B C D E F G H I
10 | A B C D E F G H I
11 | A B C D E F G H I
12 | A B C D E F G H I
13 | A B C D E F G H I
14 | A B C D E F G H I
15 | A B C D E F G H I
16 | A B C D E F G H I
17 | A B C D E F G H I
18 | A B C D E F G H I
19 | A B C D E F G H I
20 | A B C D E F G H I

21 | A B C D E F G H I
22 | A B C D E F G H I
23 | A B C D E F G H I
24 | A B C D E F G H I
25 | A B C D E F G H I
26 | A B C D E F G H I
27 | A B C D E F G H I
28 | A B C D E F G H I
29 | A B C D E F G H I
30 | A B C D E F G H I
31 | A B C D E F G H I
32 | A B C D E F G H I
33 | A B C D E F G H I
34 | A B C D E F G H I
35 | A B C D E F G H I

© UCLES K&J **Photocopiable**

158

UNIVERSITY of CAMBRIDGE
ESOL Examinations

Candidate Name
If not already printed, write name
in CAPITALS and complete the
Candidate No. grid (in pencil).

Candidate Signature

Examination Title

Centre

Supervisor:

If the candidate is ABSENT or has WITHDRAWN shade here ⟶

Centre No.

Candidate No.

Examination
Details

0	0	0	0
1	1	1	1
2	2	2	2
3	3	3	3
4	4	4	4
5	5	5	5
6	6	6	6
7	7	7	7
8	8	8	8
9	9	9	9

Candidate Answer Sheet: FCE Paper 3 Use of English

Use a PENCIL (B or HB). Rub out any answer you wish to change with an eraser.

For **Part 1**: Mark ONE letter for each question.
For example, if you think **C** is the right answer to
the question, mark your answer sheet like this:

For **Parts 2, 3, 4** and **5**: Write your answers in
the spaces next to the numbers like this:

| 0 | A | B | C̶ | D |

| 0 | example |

Part 1

1	A	B	C	D
2	A	B	C	D
3	A	B	C	D
4	A	B	C	D
5	A	B	C	D
6	A	B	C	D
7	A	B	C	D
8	A	B	C	D
9	A	B	C	D
10	A	B	C	D
11	A	B	C	D
12	A	B	C	D
13	A	B	C	D
14	A	B	C	D
15	A	B	C	D

Part 2

Do not write here

16		1 16 0
17		1 17 0
18		1 18 0
19		1 19 0
20		1 20 0
21		1 21 0
22		1 22 0
23		1 23 0
24		1 24 0
25		1 25 0
26		1 26 0
27		1 27 0
28		1 28 0
29		1 29 0
30		1 30 0

Turn
over
for
Parts
3 - 5
⟶

© UCLES K&J Photocopiable

Part 3	Do not write here
31	31 0 1 2
32	32 0 1 2
33	33 0 1 2
34	34 0 1 2
35	35 0 1 2
36	36 0 1 2
37	37 0 1 2
38	38 0 1 2
39	39 0 1 2
40	40 0 1 2

Part 4	Do not write here
41	1 41 0
42	1 42 0
43	1 43 0
44	1 44 0
45	1 45 0
46	1 46 0
47	1 47 0
48	1 48 0
49	1 49 0
50	1 50 0
51	1 51 0
52	1 52 0
53	1 53 0
54	1 54 0
55	1 55 0

Part 5	Do not write here
56	1 56 0
57	1 57 0
58	1 58 0
59	1 59 0
60	1 60 0
61	1 61 0
62	1 62 0
63	1 63 0
64	1 64 0
65	1 65 0

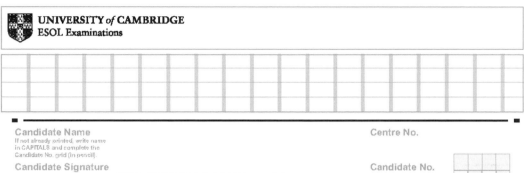

UNIVERSITY of CAMBRIDGE
ESOL Examinations

Candidate Name
If not already printed, write name
in CAPITALS and complete the
Candidate No. grid (in pencil).

Candidate Signature

Examination Title

Centre

Supervisor:
If the candidate is ABSENT or has WITHDRAWN shade here ▭

Centre No.

Candidate No.

Examination
Details

0	0	0	0
1	1	1	1
2	2	2	2
3	3	3	3
4	4	4	4
5	5	5	5
6	6	6	6
7	7	7	7
8	8	8	8
9	9	9	9

Candidate Answer Sheet: FCE Paper 4 Listening

Mark test version (in PENCIL)

A   B   C   D   E

Special arrangements   S   H

Instructions

Use a PENCIL
Rub out any answer
you wish to change
using an eraser.

For **Parts 1** and **3**:
Mark ONE letter for
each question.

For example, if you
think **B** is the right
answer to the question,
mark your answer
sheet like this:

0   A   B   C

For **Parts 2** and **4**:
Write your answers in
the spaces next to the
numbers like this:

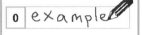

0   example

Part 1

1	A	B	C
2	A	B	C
3	A	B	C
4	A	B	C
5	A	B	C
6	A	B	C
7	A	B	C
8	A	B	C

Part 2

		Do not write here
9		1 9 0
10		1 10 0
11		1 11 0
12		1 12 0
13		1 13 0
14		1 14 0
15		1 15 0
16		1 16 0
17		1 17 0
18		1 18 0

Part 3

19	A	B	C	D	E	F
20	A	B	C	D	E	F
21	A	B	C	D	E	F
22	A	B	C	D	E	F
23	A	B	C	D	E	F

Part 4

		Do not write here
24		1 24 0
25		1 25 0
26		1 26 0
27		1 27 0
28		1 28 0
29		1 29 0
30		1 30 0